"Th[...] science, [...] power, and you will have a thread that will guide you into the labyrinth of the most impenetrable hearts."

—*Balzac*

You carry your destiny in the palm of your hand. For the various panorama of human personality are on your little palm. It, like a mirror, reflects the man and his mind from the womb to the tomb. The lines do slightly change to correspond with alterations in character.

Of your virtues and vices the palms are the true index, and Palmistry can unfold the dramatic story of career and character Kings and prophets of old devoted to the mysteries of this science.

Here is the book that answers a long-left need—a Dictionary of Palmistry, the first of its kind in India and the world, designed to meet the requirements of a beginner as well as an expert in the subject.

Thus, in arming yourself with this science, you arm yourself with a great power, and you will have a thread that will guide you into the labyrinth of the most inscrutable hearts.

—Balzac

Your very fate destiny is in the palm of your hand. For the various paramount of human personality are on your little palm. It is like a mirror, reflects the man and his mind from the womb to the tomb. The lines do slightly change to correspond with alteration in character.

Of what virtues and vices the palms are the true index, and I alone can unfold the dimmed glory of career and character—lines and prophets of old devoted to the mysteries of this science.

Here is the book that answers a long-felt need—a Dictionary of Palmistry, the first of its kind in India and this world, designed to meet the requirements of a beginner as well as an expert in the subject.

The Dictionary of Palmistry

Jagat S. Bright

JAICO PUBLISHING HOUSE
Mumbai • Delhi • Bangalore • Kolkata
Hyderabad • Chennai • Ahmedabad

Published by Jaico Publishing House
121 Mahatma Gandhi Road
Mumbai - 400 023
jaicopub@vsnl.com
www.jaicobooks.com

© Jaico Publishing House

THE DICTIONARY OF PALMISTRY
ISBN 81-7224-224-7

First Jaico Impression : 1959
Tenth Jaico Impression : 2004

No part of this book may be reproduced or utilized in
any form or by any means, electronic or
mechanical including photocopying, recording or by any
information storage and retrieval system,
without permission in writing from the publishers.

Printed by
Sanman & Co.
113, Shivshakti Ind. Estate,
Marol Naka, Andheri (E), Mumbai - 400 059.

Thus he that Nature rightly understands,
May from each line imprinted in his hands,
His future Fate and Fortune come to know,
And what Path it is his Feet shall go.
His secret Inclination he may see,
And to what Vice he shall addicted be
To th' End that when he looks into his Hand,
He may upon his Guard the better stand:
And turn his wandering steps another way:
Whene'er he finds he does from Virtue stray.

—ARISTOTLE

FOREWORD

I am indeed glad that JAICO PUBLISHING HOUSE has put before the public an invaluable guide and unique treatise on Palmistry through the publication "The Dictionary of Palmistry" by Shri Jagat S. Bright. It is a work which would be acclaimed with great delight both by amateurs as well as experts or professionals in palmistry. As a practising Astrologer and Palmist, I have for many years felt the want of this type of work which systematises the complex science of Palmistry by separating the wheat from the husk. An enthusiastic amateur gets more and more perplexed as he starts reading the available books on Palmistry, and at the end he is virtually at the beginning.

The work at once gives evidence of the great "labour of love" which Shri Jagat S. Bright has taken in compiling this book. There are numerous works on Palmistry, both Western and Oriental, protessing to deal with the entire Science of Palmistry or special parts thereof. Yet, these books do not serve the purpose of a ready-reckoner like the present "The Dictionary of Palmistry", thus losing the utility value of this science. I have been keenly watching the work of Shri Jagat S. Bright and without any hesitation or reservation feel that the present publication is an invaluable contribution to this ancient science, on which numerous works have been written by eminent personalities. Even to those professionals who have studied classic works on palmistry by Cheiro, W. G. Benham, Comte C. de Saint-Germain, A. D. Jennings, F. Kienzle, R. V. Allen and many others including the works in Sanskrit and other Indian languages, this work will gain high status due to its systematic arrangement of the various aspects of Palm Reading. Any one can put out his palm and get the rendering of every sign, pattern and trend of lines. Further, he can quickly satisfy his curiosity about any queer or exceptional formations on his palm. The book is well illustrated and written with acumen, intelligent arrangement and tact. The author has backed some of his findings and interpretations by long research and wide experience.

I heartily congratulate Shri Jagat S. Bright for his unique work which is all the more useful as he has offered an introductory chapter on the fundaments of Palmistry for the benefit of those who are new-comers. I wish Shri Bright would follow this work with a Dictionary of Astrology written on the same basis. The work speaks volumes for the easy, interesting and at the same time scientific treatment of this difficult subject, which is usually ill-used by many who put their own fanciful interpretation on the complex intricacies of lines. It is a creditable thesis and yet serves the purpose of a ready-reckoner in Palmistry. I am confident that the labours of Shri Bright would be well appreciated and welcomed by one and all and his work would be a classic contribution unparalleled by any previous publication on Palmistry, either in the East or the West. I wish him every success in his future publications and eagerly look forward to works from his pen on various other subjects. I consider it a pleasure and indeed a personal honour to have been requested to write this Foreword on a subject in which I am keenly interested both as a professional and a student. By this book Shri J. S. Bright has benefited all those who are interested in Palmistry and would even convert those who are sceptical about this science.

DR. VASANTKUMAR R. PANDIT
M.A. (Astro.) Ph.D. (Jyotish) LL.B.

PREFACE

This is not *a* book but *the* book on Palmistry. Nobody down the sweep of centuries, since Palmistry was founded, formulated and factualized, has ever attempted to reduce this branch of knowledge to a readable dictionary form. This book can safely claim to be not merely first in India but first in the world.

You can very well imagine the labour of love and the love of labour that has gone into the conception and completion of this book. The author published half a dozen hot-sellers on Palmistry anonymously before he embarked upon this venture. Even then he has quoted authorities copiously so as not to impose the entire responsibility on his own shoulders.

The book is so designed as to meet the requirements of a beginner as well as an expert in the subject. An introductory chapter has been added for the benefit of those readers who are being initiated for the first time into this fascinating lore which was fathered in the hoary past by the ancient sages of India; and like all scientific knowledge, went from East to West—and now back again!

With the help of this dictionary you can trace traits of character from signs in the hands and signs in the hand from traits of character. Many different signs and lines have been catalogued for each individual vice or virtue, so that never again should you base your predictions on solitary indications which is always a great gamble in a grand guess-work.

29/15, *Hamilton Road,*   J. S. B.
   DELHI–6.

CONTENTS

WELCOME TO PALMISTRY!

Science as well as Art	23
Panorama of Personality	24
Map of Destiny	25
The Highway of Life	26
The Signs of the Lines	27
Psychology of Palmistry	27
Fourth Dimensional Survey	29
General Impression	29
Pose of the Hands	30
Twin Sciences	30
The Rainbow of Hands	31
The Elementary Hand	31
The Square Hand	32
The Spatulate Hand	33
The Philosophic Hand	34
The Conic Hand	35
The Psychic Hand	36
The Mixed Hand	37
Light on the Hair	38
Fateful Fingers	38
Centre of the Brain	39
Nailing the Nails	40
Mounts of the Mind	40
Meeting of Mounts	41
Little Lines of Law	42
Most Important Lines	42
The Subordinate Lines are	42
Subsidiary Lines	42

11

Law of Little Lines	43
Determination of Dates	43
System of Seven	46
Distinct Divine Divisions	46
Line of Intuition	48
Can Lines Change ?	49
Significance of Handshake	49
Hollow Palm	50
Palmistry of Knots	50
Tipping the Types	51
Purpose of Palmistry	53

ALPHABETICALLY INDEXED

A

Ability, Line of	58	Apollo, Line of	62
Absence of any Main Line	58	Apollo Line, Readings from	63
Accidents	58	Apollonian Type	63
Actor	58	Apollo, Qualities of the Mounts of	63
Administrative Triangle	59	Apoplexy	64
Adventure	59	Apparatus of a Palmist	64
Adventure, Live-Dangerously	59	Architect	64
Advice, need for	59	Arm, Accident to	65
Affection, Want of	59	Arms Wounds on	65
Aggressiveness	60	Art and Science Combined	65
Agriculturist	60	Art, Failure in	65
Ague	60	Artistic Hand	65
Alcoholic Insanity	60	Artist, Very Great	65
Allahdin's Lamp	60	Assassination	66
Alternation of Events	61	Asthma	66
Ambition	61	Astronomer	66
Ambition, Political	61	Astro-Palmistry	66
Ambition without Limit	61	Audacity	67
Amorous Disposition	61	Author, Unimaginative	67
Anaemia	62	Avarice	67
Aneurism	62	Avoiding Mistakes, Capacity of	67
Anger, Habitual	62		
Animals, Affection for	62		

B

Bad Teeth	68
Bankruptcy	68
Beauty, Contempt for	68
Benevolence	68
Between Two Lovers	69
Bile and Crime	69
Bilious Headache	69
Biliousness	69
Blackmailer	69
Blackmarketing	69
Bladder Trouble	69
Blindness	70
Blood, Bad Circulation of	70
Blood, Good Circulation of	70
Bloodlessness	70
Blood Troubles	70
Bohemianism	71
Bracelets	71
Brahmacharya	71
Brain Fever	71
Brain Trouble	72
Breaks in the Lines	72
Breast, Wounds on	73
Bright's Disease	73
Brilliant Career	73
Brilliant Intellect	73
Bronchitis	73
Brute Animality	73
Bully	74
Burglar	74
Business, Aptitude for	74
Business Man, Successful	75
Business Success	75

C

Cæsar, Julius	76
Card Sharper	76
Career, Change of	76
Catarrh	76
Caution, Extreme	76
Celibacy	76
Chains, Signs from	77
Change of Lines	77
Cheirognomy and Cheiromancy	77
Chemistry, Success in	77
Childbearing Difficulties	77
Childlessness	77
Children	78
Children, Gender of	78
Circle	78
Circle on Fingers	78
Circles, Signs from	78
Clairvoyance	78
Closed Fist	79
Clubbed Thumb	79
Coarseness	79
Colour of Hand	79
Colour of Lines, Indications from	79
Colour of the Palm	79
Combativeness	80
Commercial Artist	80
Commercialization of Art	80
Compass of Hand	80
Composer of Music	80
Concentration, Lack of	81
Concentration, Power of	81
Confused Lines	81
Congenital Potentialities	81
Conquest of Love	81
Constancy	81
Constitutional Brain Trouble	82
Constitution, Strong	82
Constitution, Weak	82
Consumption, Tendency to	82
Convent Career	83
Conventionality, Excessive	83
Coquetry	83
Corruptibility	83
Courage	83
Cowardice	83
Crank, The Qualities of	84
Criminal Propensities	84
Criminal Qualities	84

Critical Faculty	85	Cross of Mental Suffering	85
Critical Illness	85	Crosses, Signs from	86
Critical Intellect	85	Cruelty, Instinctive	86
Cross	85	Cunning	87
Cross-bar	85	Curiosity	87

D

Danger Signal	88	Discontent, Habitual	92
Deafness	88	Discoveries, New	92
Death by Execution	88	Disease, Incurable	92
Death, Early	88	Disposition, Feverish	92
Death in War	88	Divisions of Hand	92
Death, Prediction of	89	Divorce	93
Death Signals	89	Dogged Determination	93
Death, Sudden and Violent	89	Domestic Disease	93
Deceitful Disposition	89	Domestic Trouble	93
Definition	90	Domineering Personality	93
Details, Love of	90	Don't-Marry Line	94
Detective Method	90	Dot	94
Devoted Love	90	Dots, Signs from	94
Diabetes	90	Double Crossing	94
Dimensions of Lines	91	Double Line of Heart	94
Diphtheria	91	Dramatic Art	94
Diplomat, Successful	91	Dramatic Genius	95
Disappointment in Ambition	91	Dreamer	95
Disappointment in Love	91	Dropsy	95
Disappointments, Life full of	92	Drowning, Danger from	95
		Drunkenness	95

E

Economy	96	Engagement, Broken	98
Effeminacy	96	Engineer's Hand	98
Egotism, Boundless	96	Envy	98
Electric Life-Current	96	Epilepsy	99
Elementary Hand	96	Events Determining Signs	99
Eloquence	97	Excitement, Temporary	99
Embezzler	97	Extravagance	99
Emotions and Mounts	97	Eye Trouble	99
Energetic Personality	98		

F

Faculty of Investigation	101	Fainting Fits	101
Failure Due to Women	101	Faithfulness	102
Failure in Art	101	Fame	102

Fame and Name	102	Fingers, General Qualities of	107
Fame, Ladder of	102	Finger Lines, Indications from	108
Family Affection	102	Fingers, Names of	108
Family Responsibility	103	Fingers, Pronounced Spacing of	108
Famous People, Hands of	103	Finger Tips Qualities of	108
Fanaticism	103	First Finger, Abnormal	109
Fatal Influence of Women	103	First Finger, Qualities of	109
Fatalism	103	Flexibility	109
Fatal Love Affair	104	Flirtation	109
Fatalistic, Palmistry is not	104	Forger	110
Fate and Fatality	104	Fork	110
Fate Line, Absence of	104	Forked Fate	110
Fate Line, Readings from	104	Formation, Chained	110
Fault-finding	105	Fourth Finger, Qualities of	110
Female Troubles	105	Friendship of the Powerful People	111
Fickle Fancy	106	Frivolity	111
Financial Failure	106	Frustration	111
Financial Instability	106	Future of Palmistry	111
Financial Trouble and Losses	106		
Finger-joints, Well formed	106		

G

Gambler, Habitual	112	Golden Rules of Palmistry	113
Gastric Fever	112	Gonorrhoea	113
Generative Functions, Troubles in	112	Good Fortune	114
Generosity, the Quadrangle of	112	Gout	114
Genius	112	Great Love	114
George Bernard Shaw, Hand of	112	Great Palmer Arch	114
Giddiness	113	Greed	115
Girdle of Venus, Readings from	113	Greta Garbo, Hand of	115
Glorious Career	113	Grille	115
		Grille, Qualities of	115
		Grill on Venus	115
		Guilty Conscience	115

H

Hair and Health	116	Hand-Reading	118
Hair, Meaning of	116	Hands, Different Kinds of	118
Hamlet	116	Handshake, Qualities of	118
Hand	116	Happiness, Domestic	118
Hand, Hair on	118	Happy Career	119

Happy-Go-Lucky Fellow	119	Hemorrhage	123
Harmony of Existence	119	Hemorrhoids	123
Hay Fever	119	Hepatica	123
Headaches	119	Hepatica, Qualities of	124
Headaches, Serious	119	Hiding Habits	124
Head, Double Line of	120	Hindu Interpretation	124
Head Line, Readings from	120	Hindu Science	125
Headstrong	121	Hollow Palm	125
Head, The Perfect	121	Honesty, Want of	125
Head, Wounds on	121	Housewife, The Excellent	125
Health Hints	121	Husband, Ideal	126
Heartlessness	121	Hydrophobia	126
Heart Line, Readings from	122	Hypersensitiveness	126
Heart Palpitations	122	Hypnotism	126
Heart Troubles	122	Hypochondriac	126
Heart Weakness	123	Hysteria	127

I

Idealism	128	Influence Lines of Life	133
Idealistic Temperament	128	Inheritance	133
Ideal Love	128	Inheritance, Rich	133
Idiocy	128	Insanity	133
Illegitimate Birth	128	Insult, Life of	134
Ill Health	129	Intellectual Ability	134
Illness	129	Intellect, Measure of	134
Illness from Love	129	Interlinked Head and Heart Lines	134
Illness from Sorrows	129	Internal Trouble	135
Illusion	129	Intestinal Trouble	135
Imagination, Creative	130	Intolerance	135
Imagination, Unhealthy	130	Intrepidity	135
Imagination with Practicality	130	Intrigues, Guilty	135
Immorality	130	Intuition, Gift of	136
Imprudence	130	Intuition, The Line of	136
Impulsiveness	131	Intuitive Power	136
Inability to Keep Secrets	131	Inventive Genius, Practical	136
Inconstancy	131	Inventive Genius, Unpractical	137
Independence of Character	131	Irony, Gift of	137
Independence of Spirit	132	Irresponsibility	137
Indigestion, Habitual	132	Irritability	137
Indomitable Determination	132	Island	137
Infantile Diseases	132	Islanded Affection Line	138
Influence, Ascending	132	Islanded Fate Line	138
Influence, Descending	132	Islanded Influence Line	138
Influence Line Influence of	132	Islanded Mercury Line	138
Influence Lines	133	Islands, Qualities of	138

J

Jack of all Trades .. 139	Judge's Hand 139
Jaundice 139	Jupiterian Type 139
Jealousy 139	Jupiter, Qualities of the Mount 140

K

Key to Character .. 141	Knotted Fingers .. 141
Kidney Trouble 141	Knotty-Fingered People .. 141

L

Lady Luck 143	Lines 148
Late Success 143	Lines, Main and Minor .. 149
Law, Success in .. 143	Lines, Minute 149
Lawyer, Qualities of .. 143	Literary Success .. 149
Laziness 143	Literature, Aptitude for .. 149
Legacies 144	Liver Line, Readings from 150
Legs, Wounds on .. 144	Liver Trouble 150
Length of Hand .. 144	Longevity 151
Length of Life .. 144	Loss of Blood 151
Lethargy .. 144	Love, Boundless .. 151
Liar .. 144	Love, Desire for .. 151
Liberality .. 145	Love Disappointed .. 151
Licentiousness .. 145	Love for a Married Person 152
Life Line, Law of 145	Love for a Near Relative 152
Life, Love-Lorn .. 145	Love for one Person Only 152
Life, Map of .. 146	Love, Happiness in .. 152
Life, Measurement of 146	Loveless Life 152
Life Readings from the Line of 146	Love Lordliest .. 152
Life, Ruined by Love .. 147	Love Without Marriage .. 152
Life, Ruined Through Imprudence 147	Lower Mars, Qualities of the Mount 153
Limpidity of Truth 147	Lunarian Type 153
Line of Longevity .. 148	Lung Disease 153
	Lust Without Love .. 153

M

Madame Curie, The Hand of 154	Main Lines Mixed .. 155
Madman, Natural .. 154	Male Sexual Trouble .. 155
Madness, Dangerous .. 154	Man of Destiny 155
Madness, Melancholy and Religious 154	Many Love Affairs .. 155
Magnetism of Mounts .. 155	Mahatma Gandhi, the Hand of 157
	Map of Life 157

Map of Mind	158
Marriage, Brilliant	158
Marriage Frustration	158
Marriage, Happy	158
Marriage Influence	158
Marriage Line, Indications from	158
Marriage, Lines of	159
Marriage, Love	159
Marriage Mismated	159
Marriage Troubles	160
Marriage, Unfit for	160
Marriage, Wealthy	160
Marriage with an Artist	160
Marriage with an Old Person	160
Marriage with a Trader	160
Mars, the Line of	161
Martian Type	161
Material Love	161
Maternity, Danger of	161
Mathematician's Hand	161
Meanness	162
Measurements	162
Mechanical Aptitude	162
Mechanical Powers	162
Medical Profession	163
Medical Stigmata	163
Mediocrity	163
Melancholia	163
Memory, Bad	164
Memory, Good	164
Memory, Loss of	164
Mercenary Mental Make up	164
Mercenary Soldier	164
Mercurian Type	165
Mercury, Line of	165
Mercury, Qualities of the Mount of	165
Military Honours	165
Military Mind	165
Misanthrope	166
Miserly Mind	166
Mixed Hand	166
Moodiness	166
Moon, Qualities of the Mount of	166
Moons on the Nails	167
Moral Depravity	167
Morbid Disposition	167
Morbidness, Oversensitive	168
Mounts, Location of	168
Mounts, Meaning of	168
Mount, Presence of	169
Mount Type	169
Much-Ado-About-Nothing Mentality	169
Murderer for Profit	169
Murderer, the Slow	169
Murderer, Treacherous	170
Murderer, Very Habitual	170
Murderer, Violent	170
Musical Genius	171
Musical Instrumentalists	171
Musical Man	171
Musician's Hand	171
Mystic Cross	171

N

Nails	172
Nails, Good	172
Nails, Indications from	172
Nails, Qualities of	173
Nails Perfect	173
Napoleon's Index	173
Naval Profession	173
Negative Existence	173
Nervous Trouble	173
Neuralgia	174
Nurse	174

O

Observation, Importance of	175
Obstinacy	175
Occult Sciences, Aptitude for	175
Officiousness	175
Old Age	176
Opera Singer	176
Opposite Sex, Influence of	176
Optimistic Hand-Reading	176
Ordinary Illness	176
Organic Affection	177
Origin of Palmistry	177
Other People, Influence of	177
Overdoing Luck	177
Over-indulgence	177
Overworked Intellect	178

P

Painter	179
Palmist	179
Palmist, Qualities of	179
Palmistry	179
Palm, Qualities of	180
Palpitation of the Heart	180
Paralysis	181
Passionate Crime	181
Perseverance	181
Personal Magnetism	181
Pessimism, Literary	181
Pets, Love for	181
Philosophic Knot	181
Philosopher	182
Physician	182
Pickpocket	182
Pictures, Palmistry in	183
Pleurisy	183
Poetical Power	183
Pointed Angle	183
Politician	184
Poverty	184
Predetermination	184
Prediction About Life	184
Pride, Indomitable	185
Priesthood	185
Prints of Hands	185
Prison Life	186
Profession, Choice of	186
Profligacy	186
Prophet-Mongering	186
Prostration, Nervous	186
Prudence	187
Psychic Hand	187
Psychology of Hand	187
Public Honours	188

Q

Quadrangle	189

R

Rashness	190
Rays of Influence	190
Reading, Love of	190
Reciprocated Affection	190
Reflection	190
Relatives, Influence of	190
Relatives on the Line of Apollo	191
Religion	191
Reverses of Fortune	191
Rheumatism	191
Robber, The Highway	191
Romance	192
Romantic Madness	192
Romantic Nature	192
Roseate Health	193
Roosevelt, Hand of	193

S

Sadness, Imaginary	194
Satin Skin	194
Saturnian Type	194
Saturn, Line of	194
Saturn, Qualities of the Mount	194
Saturn, the Ring of	195
Scandal	195
Scarlet Fever	195
Scholar's Hand	195
Science and Art Combined	196
Science of Palmistry	196
Science, Success in	197
Scientific Genius	197
Sculptor	198
Second Finger, Qualities of	198
Seers, Sages and Saints	198
Self-Abuse	199
Self-confidence	199
Self-contained Individual	199
Self-Importance	199
Selfishness, Excessive	199
Self-Made Man	199
Self-Projection	200
Self-Reform	200
Sensitiveness	200
Sensitiveness to Criticism	200
Sensuality	200
Sex Sublimation	201
Sign of Death	201
Sister Life-Line	201
Sister Lines	201
Sixth Sense	201
Size of the Hands	202
Skill in Love	202
Skin, Climate of	202
Slippery Fellow	202
Smartness	202
Soldier's Hand	202
Solomon, The Ring of	203
Somnambulism	203
Space Between Life and Head	203
Space Signs	203
Spatulate Hand	204
Speculator's Hand	204
Speculator, Successful	204
Spendthrift Disposition	204
Spinal Trouble	205
Spiritual Inclination	205
Sportsmanship	205
Square	205
Square Hand	205
Squares, Signs from	206
Star	206
Star of Brilliant Intellect	206
Star of Tragic Fate	206
Star of Unusual Faculties	207
Stars, Signs from	208
Statesmanship	208
Sterility	208
Stock-broker's Hand	209
Stoicism	209
Stomach Trouble	209
Striking a Balance	209
Subconscious Mind	209
Success by Chance	209
Successful Ambitious Career	210
Successful Clerk	210
Success in Arts	210
Success, Line of	210
Success, Signs of	210
Success through Hard Work	211
Suicidal Mania	211
Suicidal Tendencies	211
Suicide	211
Sunstroke	212
Superstition	212
Surgeon's Hand	212
Suspicion	212
Swindler	212
Syphilis	212

T

Tact 214	Thumb, Importance of .. 219
Talent Abused 214	Thumb Lines, Readings from 221
Talking of Palmistry .. 214	Thumb, Qualities of .. 221
Talking of Talent .. 215	Time, Determination of .. 222
Tassel 215	Timidity 222
Teaching Profession .. 215	Tips and Knots, Indications from 222
Teeth Trouble 215	Tragedy, Comic .. 222
Telepathic Powers .. 216	Traitor 223
Temper, Evenness of .. 216	Traveller, Habitual .. 223
Temper Test 216	Travel Lines 223
Temporary Mental Derangement 216	Triangle 223
Tendencies 216	Triangle of Ready Wit .. 224
Texture of Fingers .. 216	Triangle, Smaller .. 224
Thickness of Hand, Qualities of 217	Triangles, Signs from .. 224
Thief 217	Triangle, The Great .. 224
Third Finger, Qualities of 217	Trident 225
Thoughtless Disposition 218	Troubles in Love .. 225
Thought-Reading .. 218	Troubles in Manhood .. 225
Three Worlds of Palmistry 218	Tumour, Cancer .. 225
Throat Trouble 218	Typhoid 225
Thumb 219	Tyrannical D position .. 225
Thumb, Divisions of .. 219	

U

Unconventionality .. 226	Unsociability 226
Unhappiness through Women 226	Unusual Shrewdness .. 227
Unhappy Marriages, Prevention of 226	Upper Mars, Qualities of the Mount of .. 227

V

Vacillation 228	Via Lasciva 230
Vanity 228	Via Lasciva, Readings from 230
Variations of Hand .. 228	Vice 231
Vegetative Existence .. 229	Vindictiveness .. 231
Venereal Disease .. 229	Violent Nature 231
Venus, Girdle of .. 229	V.I.P. Friendships .. 231
Venusian Type 229	Visionary 231
Venus, Qualities of the Mount of 230	Voyages, Lucky .. 232
Versatility 230	Voyages, Unlucky .. 232

W

Wavering Mind	233
Wealth and Honour	233
Where Cupid Dwells	233
Whole and Sole Love	233
Wickedest Vice	233
Whorls	234
Widowhood	235
Windfall	235
Wit and Humour	235
Woman-Behind-Man Power	235
Woodrow Wilson, Hand of	236
World of Childhood	237
Wounds	237
Wounds, Dangerous	237
Wounds in a Fight	237
Wounds in Vital Organs	237
Wounds, Mortal	237

WELCOME TO PALMISTRY

Palmistry paves the path to pleasure, profit and power. For pleasure it is the best of the hobbies. For profit it can help you earn a decent living if you apply yourself studiously to it. For power you can rule over the hearts of peoples and politicians by knowing their weaknesses and strengths. Little wonder, every year Palmistry is making countless converts who turn to it for faith, fate, fame and fortune in their best and the worst of hours.

Science as well as Art

Palmistry is a science as well as an art. It is the oldest of arts and the youngest of science. It is the youngest of arts and the oldest of sciences. It is not possible to demarcate its frontiers, because its scope is ever-widening on the basis of fresh-flowing facts. All deductions are based on physiological and psychological premises. Even a layman finds that Palmistry is logical and lucid, interesting as well as instructive.

One must study the hand very carefully before drawing conclusions. He must use his brain like an expert criminologist. The very ridges of the skin and colour of the hair give out precious clues to the occult detective of Palmistry. The lines and signs in the hands have fascinated the saints, sages and scientists down the centuries. Thus Sir Thomas Browne in his *Religio Medici* referred to Palmistry as follows:—

"Now there are besides these characters in our faces certain mystical figures in our hands, which I dare not call mere dashes, strokes *ala volee* or at random, because delineated by a pencil that never works in vain, and hereof I take more particular notice, because I carry that in mine own hand which I could never read nor discover in another."

Apart from the philosophers, the scientists, have offered their own rationale. Each brain cell is an electric dynamo. Energy generated by the brain cells in the fluid form of ideas and ideals is recorded on the graph of the palms. According to Meissner, the distribution of corpuscles in the hand is astounding: in the finger-tips there are 108 to the square line with 400 papillae. Little wonder, the finger-tips and the nails, which are nerve-ends, play a vital role in the Science of Palmistry.

"The line where flesh ends and nail begins", says Balzac, "contains the inexplicable mystery of the constant transformation of fluids into horn, showing that nothing is impossible to the wonderful modifications of the human substance."

A science thoroughly grounded in reason, Palmistry can unfold the dramatic story of career and character. Even the kings and prophets devoted themselves to the mysteries of this science. Both Alexander and Julius Caesar were its ardent devotees. Biblical history is full of predictions based on readings of human features. The ancient sages studied the human hand as meticulously as we study the machines. "The study", said Alexander the Great, " is worth the while of an elevating and inquiring mind."

Panorama of Personality

On the landscape of the palm one can study the vast panorama of human personality. The human hand strikes the keynote of the cosmic soul. Palmistry gives us a penetrating discernment of individual character. The palm, like a mirror, reflects the man and his mind from the womb to the tomb. It is a fascinating hobby as well as a precious profession. After a little systematic study one comes to the inescapable conclusion that the lines on the palm are a "Word-

Portrait of the individual. The Art of the Interpretation of Hands is an astonishing asset in the market of life and living. Much more scientifically valuable than a photograph is the sculptured replica of the hands.

Palm is an infallible index to personality. As on a graph of flesh it records convulsions of the brain. In the case of men, lines of the left hand indicate mental and cultural inheritance, while those of the right show the accomplishment and mental development. The reverse is the case with women. The ridges on fingers and palms seldom change. That is why, the system of personal identification by fingerprints is universally recognised. The hands of a new-born babe are almost fully marked. He carries his destiny in the palm of his hand. The lines do slightly change to correspond with alterations in character. If a man really changes, the map of his palm will change completely. On the whole we do remain slaves to our predetermined fate and fortune, as Shakespeare said:

> *There's a divinity that shapes our ends,*
> *Rough-hew them how we will.*

Map of Destiny

The two hands of a friend or foe open the map of his destiny before you. They are wonderful indications of the inner self. They are the true index of our virtues and vices. Palmistry is the best way to pierce the veil that conceals the future. It satisfies the ceaseless yearning of the humans towards the unfathomable.

"The lines of the hand", says Alice Denton Jennings in *Your Hand Tells All*, "change only under the influence of the mind, the will, the emotions, and particularly under the deep-reaching influence of disease. It is these impressions which result in the birth of the little accessory lines which attach themselves to the main lines, bar or impede them, as well as form figures of various kinds . . . crosses, squares, triangles, dots, islands, etc. The shape of the hand never changes."

Palmistry today is a marvellous edifice. It borrows its stones from the ancient civilizations of all lands. The Hindu sages were the first who brought a rich lore to the treasure-house of palmistrical information. Palmistry traces its mysteries to the stars and their magnetic influence on the denizens of the earth. The magnificence of its meaning and mission incontestably issues from the far-off heavenly splendour.

"Around the man's nerves", wrote Alexander Von Humboldt, "there does exist an invisible atmosphere."

The Highway of Life

Palmistry is the Highway of Life Like all other sciences it employs observation experiment, comparison and analogy to arrive at the truth. It marches forward by the common method of trial and error. Concentration of mind is the very ABC of this science. Its laws are founded on the rock-bottom of experience. Even a hurried study can yield rich fruits and spur you to further and farther action. A perusal of the hand is a key to the personality A spirit of enquiry is the guiding principle of all sciences. Palmistry also demands this form of application. The human hand is a magnificent instrument capable of rich diversity of purposes.

Do not skip over small details in order to hit highlights. Small dots and dashes provide a wealth of information for the formulation of a correct judgment. Study the whole geography of the hands before determining the climate of character. In all considerations the thumb is the most important. It is like the Mount Everest presiding over the Indo-Gangetic Plain.

The next in importance are the mounts or fleshy cushions below the fingers. In reading mounts, do not fail to locate the apex. It is the little tripod or triangular formation in the skin lines. A little study and experience will give you confidence in the understanding of the mounts. Having surveyed the landscape, study the river-line of geography on the palm of personality. Coarse lines indicate a nature lacking in cultural refinement.

The Signs of the Lines

Remember that Head Line is the most outstanding mark on the hand. Double lines show double qualities, vices as well as virtues. Heart Line dipping towards the Head Line indicates a tendency of sentiments to be regulated by reason. One indication may be cancelled out by the other. For example, flexibility *Change* of the thumb modifies the cruelty of the Heart Line.

"People who have the circle formation on their finger-tips are always eager to finish what they start."

Everywhere let your logic be tempered with the milk of human kindness. Do not hurt anybody unnecessarily. Remember that there is a great gulf between prediction and realization. A great goodwill alone can build a golden bridge across it. Try to fix up career and character rather than launching forth into the shadow of tragic events like danger, death or disaster.

"There is no doubt", says Josef Ranald, "that this science is of eminently practical value in the choice of a vocation."

Always take time to formulate your judgment. Take a person alone and brood over his palm. Palmistry is only a pathway to light which springs from within. Look out for the mountains of might rather than the vales of weakness. Rather try to locate a tiny brook of milk than a river of poison.

Psychology of Palmistry

Never belittle the psychology of Palmistry. Whatever you are going to tell a person, right or wrong, it will influence his career and character. Call a man a thief and he will steal. If you predict the death of a trusty friend, he may die on the appointed day. By predicting goodness, you put a premium upon goodness. Do not hasten evil by forecasting it. Do not think that I debar you from telling the truth. Do goodness with a grace. One may tell a lie truly and speak the truth falsely. Right impression must be matched with a right expression. Remember that a sweet dish served harshly tastes bitter. On the contrary, we enjoy a bitter medicine served nicely by a nurse.

Do not leap to your conclusions. There are always neutralizing factors which must not be ignored. Scientific work is always painfully slow but it is always richly fruitful. Captain d'Arpentigny, who fought many battles under Napoleon, spent many hours to co-ordinate his results of the study of hands. Napoleon believed in Palmistry. So did Hitler. The works of Arpentigny were printed in 1943. These are wonderful documents of study and insight.

A palmist, like a painter, brings his intuition into play. Without intuition one cannot become perfect in any science or art. Intuition is essential to reach the Inner Personality of the subject. Prediction is a very illusive thing. It can only be located through intuition. The essence of destiny lies in the spirit.

"The brain which admittedly houses the mind", says Rita Van Alen, "is intimately related with the hand—its most constant servant—that from this point alone, it may be realized that the hand outwardly reflects the personality more revealingly than any other part of the anatomy."

The hand is a mirror of the mind. The nerve fluid accounts for the lines on the hand. The flowers of future potentialities also grow in the palm of the hand. There is a strange mysterious language in the hunches of the hand. A palmist must cultivate the habit of mental introspection. That way alone he can reach up to the unexplored depths of mind. There he will find the kaleidoscopic personality which cannot be summarized in sweeping generalizations.

Fourth Dimensional Survey

"Time is not an item on the map", says Rita Van Alen, "Past, Present and Future are not depicted on any automobile map, although they would be necessarily present on any trip. This map is an over-all view merging time and distance. Similarly if the panorama of one's life were imprinted on some level of the mind, one might call it a fourth dimensional survey of one's entire life and experience. But that part of the mind which is without natural limitations must be vividly aware too, that the personal journey is but the minutest fragment of a line inextricably blended into a map immense enough to contain all the billions of contemporaneous life and journeys. What a mysterious map indeed, charting the way for the great march of humanity towards an undisclosed destination."

General Impression

The thing to note is the general impression of the hand as you scan an architectural edifice and make your deductions:—

1. People with large hands are fond of details and people with small hands are only interested in the big design of life, business, etc.

2. Soft hands are ruled by imagination and belong to the class of artists, while men with hard hands are practical workers.

3. A thin hand shows timidity, meanness and poverty of intellect. A thick hand belongs to the labourer.

4. A very hollow hand indicates a financial failure.

5 Cold hands indicate a reserved and unemotional

nature. Warm hands show vivacity and personal magnetism.

6. A medium-sized hand shows coolness in emergency.

7. A dead-white hand shows lack of ardour. A pink hand indicates a gentle and sympathetic spirit. Red hands show ardour and intensity.

8. A wet hand shows warm-bloodedness and vivacity of spirits. A dry hand indicates lack of spirits and enthusiasm.

Pose of the Hands

1. When a person keeps his hands as closed as possible, he has a dark side to his character.

2. When the hand hangs down naturally but the fingers are partially closed, the person is cautious but trustworthy.

3. When the fists are firmly closed, it indicates a bully.

4. A person who carries his hands awkwardly up and down betrays an uncertainty of purpose.

5. A person who waves his hands purposefully betrays caution and watchfulness.

6. Toying with hanky, watch, button, etc. betrays a temporary excitement.

7. Hands clasped in front show a calm and quiet temperament.

8. Rubbing hands together shows an untruthful and hypocritical temperament.

9. Hands clasped behind show extreme caution.

Twin Sciences

Palmistry is scientifically classified into the twin sciences of Cheirognomy and Cheiromancy.

Cheirognomy concerns itself with the shape of the hand and fingers. Hereditary influences are also grouped under this head.

Cheiromancy deals with the lineography of the hand and also concerns itself with events of the past, present and future.

The Rainbow of Hands

There are seven types of hands like the seven colours of a rainbow:—

1. The Elementary Hand.
2. The Square Hand.
3. The Spatulate Hand.
4. The Philosophic Hand.
5. The Conic Hand.
6. The Psychic Hand.
7. The Mixed Hand

(1) *The Elementary Hand*

It is often of the clubbed type with a short clumsy thumb and stiff heavy fingers. "This hand", says Cheiro, "naturally belongs to the lowest type of mentality."

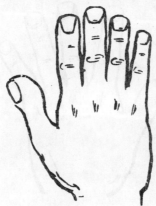

Elementary Hand

These hands undertake unskilled manual labour. Their daily routine is carried out by the dimmest flickerings of instinct. To these hands belong war and colonization. Their opinions are formed in a groove. Their virtues are of a negative nature. But they love music.

(2) *The Square Hand*

The Square Hand is the hand of practicality. It has a square appearance as a whole and its finger-tips are also square. It has a large thumb and the palm too looks square. It is a hand of patience, foresight and hardiness of spirit. It also indicates conventionality and love of order. The square-handed people are obedient to authority. They walk miles rather than trespass on somebody's property.

A square-handed person has many useful qualities "He obeys the law", says Henry Frith, "not the man.' He is neat and tidy. He is courteous and looks well

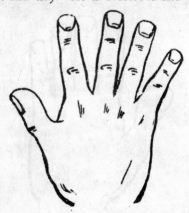

Square Hand

dressed even in torn clothes. In religion he is likely to go to the extremes. He prefers dogma to ideas.

(3) *The Spatulate Hand*

The nailed phalanges of the hand give the appearance of more or less flattened-out spatula. These hands have large thumbs. Manual labour with a sense of adventure is agreeable to them. Their self-confidence is extreme. They are valiant workers. They are leaders in arts of peace and war.

"Their love of locomotion", says d'Arpentigny, "renders them comparatively insensible to the annoyance of expatriation. Wherever they are in majority, as is the case in England and the United States, liberty in its broadest meaning, is the base of all political institutions, a fact which does not prevent, but rather

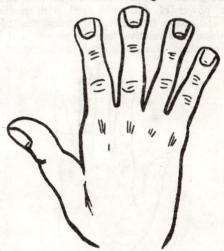

Spatulate Hand

prove, that of all nations in the world, the English and the Americans are the most prone to exclusiveness and individuality."

(4) The Philosophic Hand

The palm is large and well-formed The fingers are knotty. The nailed phalanges are half-square and half-conical. The upper knot of fingers looks like an egg-shaped spatula. They are athirst for true knowledge. When the hands are large, they incline towards analysis. When the hands are small, they incline towards synthesis. When the thumb is small, they are guided by the heart. When the thumb is big, they are dominated by the head.

"By their knots", says d'Arpentigny," philosophical hands are gifted with calculation, with a more or less vigorous power of deduction and with methods in thought and action; by their quasi-conical tips they have the intuition of a relative form of poetry; and by the whole formation of combinations including of course

Philosophic Hand

the thumb, they have the instinct of metaphysics. They plunge into the outer as well as into the inner world, but they seek less after the form than after the essence of things, less after beauty than after truth."

(5) *The Conic Hand*

The Conic or the Artistic Hand has fingers slightly tapering at the end. The hand is supple and soft. Palm is of moderate size. The thumb is rather small.

"Its owner", says Henry Frith, "is impulsive, imaginative, a lover of the beautiful, rather self-indulgent and because of his smooth, conic, rather thick fingers, likes to enjoy himself."

A conic hand has nails like cones or elongated thimbles. These persons are experts in artistic affairs, like painting, sculpture, poetry, music, etc. Imagination is their main playfield. They are men of sentiments rather than ideas. They appreciate colour more than the form. They have an imagination of fire and heart of ice. Napoleon had a conical hand.

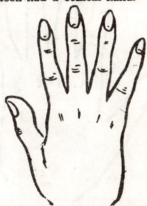

Conic or Artistic Hand

"Generals with Conical Hands", writes d'Arpentigny, "proceed by inspiration, and move by sallies; they are gifted with prowess, promptitude, passionate instincts, boastfulness, and the talent of being impromptu; they attach more importance to passing glory than to solid durable work."

(6) *The Psychic Hand*

"This is the most beautiful hand of all", says Henry Frith, "but it is not useful. The fingers are very conic, almost pointed and the hand is small, delicate, smooth and tapering. The upper phalanges are long in proportion and the lowest (also in proportion) rather thickened. Idealism and love of ease are combined in them. The owners of such hands love beauty, are ethereal and imaginative."

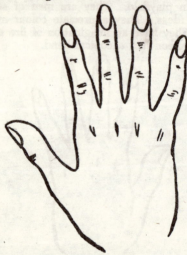

Psychic Hand

These people are poetic and enthusiastic but also nervous. They are children of impulse. They look for imagination and art everywhere. They look for divine reason. They pay no attention to form. They make good mediums in the materialization of spirits. They are gilded in the sunray of eternal life. People put them upon the pedestal and open their hearts to them for knowledge of the life beyond.

(7) *The Mixed Hand*

These hands are indistinguishable mixtures of two

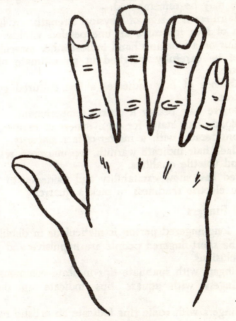

Mixed Hand

or more types. Finger-tips and palms do not belong to any specific type. It combines the good and bad characteristics of both or all. It is the hand of ideas. It is the hand of versatility. Changeability of purpose is its most essential characteristic. The person is clever but erratic in the application of his talents. He is inclined to become a Jack of all trades.

Light on the Hair

A study of hair becomes important when complex characters have to be unlocked. The following characteristics may be remembered:—

1. Hairiness is a sign of physical strength. A liberal growth of hair indicates an unexpended vitality.

2. Hair on a woman's hand indicates her masculinity. It must be carefully weighed in an estimate of her character.

3. Absence of hair indicates a fine cultured gentlemanliness.

4. Coarse hair betray a coarse temperament.

5. Blonde hair stand for an evenness of temper, cool and considerate, with a matter-of-fact sincerity.

6. Black hair indicate warmth, sensuousness, restlessness and volatile qualities.

7. Red hair show excitability and tendency to "flare up", an electric readiness to pick a quarrel.

Fateful Fingers

1. A long-fingered person is meticulous in details.

2. The short-fingered people are impulsive and jump to conclusions.

3. Fingers with spatulate tips indicate commonsense.

4. Fingers with square tips indicate an orderly mind.

5. Fingers with conic tips indicate an artistic nature.

6. Persons with pointed tips build an ivory tower in

a rose garden. That is to say, they are more imaginative and less practical.

7 Fingers set at slightly curved angle indicate clear thinking and clear sailing.

8. If the fingers are set low, it indicates a loss of power.

9. The finger of Mercury set low indicates a heartbreak in life.

10. Long Jupiter finger shows a love of authority and power to sway people

11. A short finger of Jupiter indicates non-aggressiveness and contempt of authority.

12. Stiff fingers betray an inflexibility of character.

13. Thick fingers indicate materialistic appetites.

14. Suppleness of fingers is a sign of tact and diplomacy.

15. Flattened fingers indicate an ascetic nature.

Centre of the Brain

With or without ample justification, Thumb has been called "Centre of the Brain . The thumb individualizes the man. The better proportioned the thumb, the greater the intellectual qualities.

"The most significant of all", says Cherio, "is that which relates to what is known in medical work as the 'thumb centre' of the brain. It is well-known among the specialists of nervous diseases that by the examination of the thumb they can tell if the patient is affected, or is likely to be affected, by paralysis or not, as thumb will indicate such a likelihood a long time before there has appeared the slightest trace of such a disease in any part of the system. If it indicates such an affection, an operation is at once performed on the thumb centre of the brain, and if that operation is successful (which is again shown by the thumb) they have baffled the disease and the patient is saved."

Nailing the Nails

A correct study of nails is a sure index of death, disease and mental dangers. Medical men in Paris and London pay a special attention to the study of nails.

1. Small flat nails indicate a danger of heart disease.
2. Fluted nails are indicators of lung delicacy.
3. Short well-formed nails show a faculty for criticism.
4. Filbert nails show up a visionary.
5. Long-nailed people are idealistic in temperament.
6. Brittle nails show laryngitis, asthma, catarrh and bronchial affection.
7. Triangular nails indicate a tendency to paralysis.
8. Ribbed nails indicate scrofulla and consumption.

Mounts of the Mind

There are slight elevations that wreathe the palm. These are called Mounts and depict deeply-embedded qualities of the mind. There are eight Mounts on the hand; but all are not found upon every hand:—

1. Mount of Jupiter—at the root of the first finger.
2. **Mount of Saturn**—beneath the second finger.
3. Mount of Sun or Apollo—under the third finger.
4. Mount of Mercury—at the base of the fourth finger.
5. Mount of Moon or Luna—it is near the wrist just above the first bracelet of the Rascette.
6. Mount of Venus—it encloses the root of the thumb.
7. Upper Mount of Mars—between the Lines of Head and Life or near about.
8. Lower Mount of Mars—between the little finger and the Mount of Moon.

All these mounts have individual qualities which you can find out in this "Dictionary of Palmistry" under their respective heads.

Meeting of Mounts

1. When the Mounts of Jupiter and Saturn rise above all other Mounts, it is an assurance of good luck throughout life.
2. When the Mounts of Jupiter and Apollo predominate, it is a good prognostic of wealth and reputation.

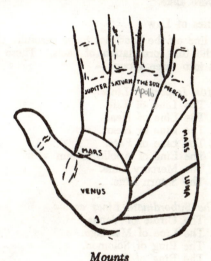

Mounts

3. Love of exact sciences is indicated by the mastery of Jupiter and Mercury.
4. An indication of cheerfulness is signalized by the combination of Jupiter and Venus.
5. A combination of Saturn and Apollo shows a good heart and a good taste.
6. A combination of Saturn and Mercury indicates a love of the mysterious and efficiency in occult sciences.

7. A predominance of Venus and Moon indicates a romantic love affair.

"There is an age-old theory" says Rita Van Alen, "that in the beginning all humanity was divided into seven parts, and each part was made up of individuals of a distinct type. The habits and attributes, and even physical appearance of each person in a typical group, were alike."

Little Lines of Law

Every line on the hand has to be carefully considered for the full formulation of facts. These can be classified into three groups.—

I. *Most Important Lines:—*
   1. The Line of Life.
   2. The Line of Head.
   3. The Line of Heart.
   4. The Line of Fate.
   5. The Line of Apollo or Sun
   6. The Mercury Line.
   7. The Saturn Line.

II. *The Subordinate Lines are:—*
   1. The Cirdle of Venus.
   2. The Line of Marriage.
   3. The Ring of Solomon.
   4. The Ring of Saturn.
   5. The Bracelets.
   6. The Line of Intuition.
   7. The Line of Mars.

III. *Subsidiary Lines:—*
   1. Lines marking the mounts.
   2. Lines of Ascending influence.
   3. Lines of Descending influence.
   4. Lines of Emergency.

5. Lines on the fingers.
6. Lines on the Thumb.
7. Lines of Travel.

These lines are explained and expounded in the body of this book and you should look out for their implications and applications under appropriate respective heads.

Law of Little Lines

1. Pale lines indicate want of robust health and lack of energy.

2. Rosy lines are the signs of roseate health.

3. Yellow lines indicate biliousness and liver trouble.

4. Dark lines indicate a proud and melancholy temperament.

5. All the lines and mounts must be taken into cool consideration before passing a judgment.

6. A sister line strengthens the main line. A break in both the lines confirms the evil nature of the break.

7. When the hand is covered with a network of confused lines, it is an indication of confused existence.

8. A trident is a three-pronged spear-head. It adds strength and brilliance.

9. The map of the hand must be studied coolly and carefully.

"To be able to read the hand is to be able to read the secret book of nature, that volume whose pages are human Life and Death, and whose clasp is the golden thread of hope that runs through all men's lives."

Determination of Dates

Determination of dates regarding an event in the future is the most difficult, not very reliable and should in no case be attempted by a beginner. Cheiro did sometimes give the dates, but even there it is doubtful whether he was always successful. Nevertheless, it is most fascinating and there is no harm if you make an attempt for your own satisfaction rather than to convince the subject. Let it be firmly borne in mind that exact dates cannot be determined by any known system of modern Palmistry. Those who have been able to predict events exactly, it was either fluke or occult power but certainly not an application of a palmistrical rules.

Dates can be determined both on the Line of Life and the Line of Fate. These two lines intersect most of the other lines. Most of the mounts are connected with these lines through rays of influence. Consequently these lines should be used for dating your destiny from womb to the tomb. But practice is the most essential factor. Without practice you are not likely to get any nearer the truth. The size of the hand should also be taken into account. Proper allowance must be made for long slender hands. Experience alone will give you the "sure look that will divide the Lines of Life and Fate into properly-sized sections without any other compasses than the pair we possess in our eyes."

One method has been given in the book under the heading "Life, Measurement of". Study it and follow it up for practice. You can apply the same method to the Line of Fate. Measure with a thread from the first bracelet to the root of the second finger. If the Line of Fate is very small, it does not matter. All the same, you go up to the root of the second finger. Fold the thread up to the Head Line from the wrist into three parts and mark the points. Dates are as follows:—

End of the first section	5th year.
End of the second section	19th year.
End of the third section	35th year.

These sections are to be applied only to the part up to the Fate Line joining the Head Line. Only this much of portion should be divided into three parts. After this you make up like this:—

Where the Fate Line joins the Heart
Line .. .. 35th year.
Where the Fate Line joins the Heart
Line .. .. 50th year.
Where the Fate Line joins the root
of the second finger .. .. 70th year.

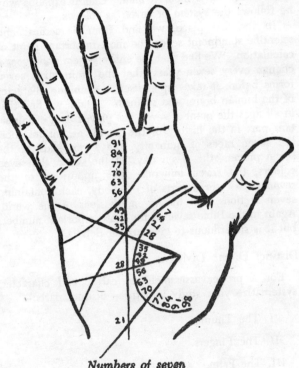

Numbers of seven

System of Seven

Cheiro follows a system of seven. Measure the Life Line or the Fate Line with a thread and then divide it into seven parts, as described above, and mark the line accordingly. Every part will represent ten years so as to make seventy years, the traditional span of life for a modern man. Cheiro explains why he follows the system of seven as follows:—

"In the first place, we find from a medical and scientific standpoint seven the most important point of calculation. We find that the entire system undergoes a change every seven years; that the brain takes seven forms before it takes upon itself the unique character of the human brain; and so forth. Again, we find that in all ages the number seven has played a most important part in the history of the world; as, for instance, the seven races of humanity, the seven gods of the seven planets, the seven days of the week, the seven colours, the seven minerals, the supposition of the seven senses, three parts of the body, each containing seven sections, and the seven divisions of the world. Again in the Bible seven is the most important number; but it is superfluous to give further details."

Distinct Divine Divisions

For a proper assessment of career and character, systematize your study into three distinct parts:—

I. The Thumb

II. The Fingers.

III. The Palm.

THE DICTIONARY OF PALMISTRY

All these three are equally important and supplement one another. If you merely fix your mind on lines and mounts, you are likely to go astray, because much mystery is hidden in the fingers. As to the thumb, it

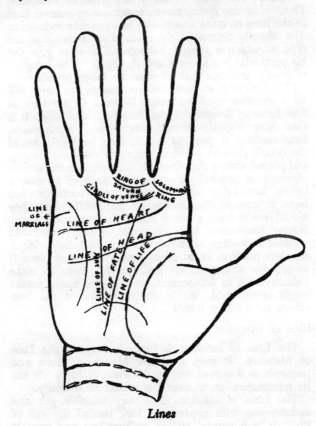

Lines

alone is sufficient to provide a complete clue to the mind of a man unsupported by any other evidence.

Only when you grasp these three Distinct Divine Divisions, you come to know the ABC of Palmistry. There is no use giving more importance to mounts than to the lines or more importance to lines than to mounts. The Mounts determine the main characteristics of the type to which a subject belongs. The lines give out his particular weaknesses and strengths. The integrated study demands that all must be taken together.

"That there is so much information in the hand will be a surprise to many," says William G. Benham in *The Laws of Scientific Hand Reading,* "and when it is seen how logical, rational, and even commonplace, hand-reading is, perhaps it will then be taken out of the occult class to which it distinctly does not belong, and placed among the other rational means at the service of mankind, whereby they may be enabled to gain a better knowledge of themselves. My ambition has been to present this matter to the public, that they would see it from a novel point of view, and by disclosing the logical basis on which it rests, presented without a vestige of mysticism or occult help, lift it from its position as an effete superstition, and place it among the sciences. My ambition has been to make Palmistry not an amusement, nor a centre where cranks might congregate, but a study worthy of the best efforts of the best minds."

Line of Intuition

The Line of Intuition is located alongside the Line of Mercury. It rises from the Mount of Moon and proceeds in a curved way to the Plain of Mars. It has its termination on or near the Mount of Mercury.

The Line of Intuition is a very valuable gift and endows one with capacity to look behind the veil of life. It is a special gift of philosophers and psychic persons. Whatever the person says, even if in joke, it is likely to come to be true. His life is so much in tune with the supernatural that he can see the future as the present.

The degree of intuition is negligible if the line is islanded. If the Line of Intuition gets entangled with the Head Line, the intuitive powers are likely to be hampered by excessive imagination. If an influence line joins the Mount of Jupiter with the Line of Intuition, it will be highly instrumental in the realization of one's ambitions. With a clear Line of Intuition one can become a great occultist, medium fortune-teller, clairvoyant, etc.

Can Lines Change?

Yes, the lines can change but not so easily as you may think. You can change your lines by changing your character. You can change your character only through a very great effort of will. It is believed by most of the palmists that some changes do take place every seven years; but usually these are not very significant alterations. These are mostly influence lines that creep up here and there to neutralize the evil effects or strengthen the good results.

"People do not change their typical qualities until they have a strong desire to change, and are armed with a resolution to do it. Thus it seems that there is no greater truth than that we are indeed free agents, planned for a predestined destiny, but always able to change it if we determinedly desire to do so. There is, then, no such thing as absolute fatalism."

Significance of Handshake

A handshake provides a valuable clue to the character of the person with whom you are dealing. "The handshake" says Frances Kienzle, "is the first index to a person's character. Don't you often form an opinion of a person by the manner in which he shakes your hand? If it is possible to shake hands with a person whose hands you wish to read, it will reveal a great deal about him."

People with soft and flabby hands have a negative character. They love luxury but do not exert themselves to be pleasant to others. Soft palm shows self-indulgence. Such a person is governed by a strong imagination. Flabby hands indicate heartlessness. The possessor has a glib tongue but he is fundamentally insincere.

A dutiful, dependable and disciplined person is one who has a firm handshake. The hard hand denotes a practical character. A hurting handshake betrays an extremist character of strong likes and dislikes.

"The firm hand that has resiliency is the ideal hand. The person with such a hand is ambitious, energetic and enjoys the happy medium disposition."

Hollow Palm

A hollow palm shows falls and pitfalls, defeats and disappointments. Inclining towards the Line of Life, a hollow palm indicates domestic disappointments. Leaning towards the Line of Heart, it betrays failure in affections. "A hollow palm", says Cheiro, 'has been proved to be an unfortunate sign; such people usually have even more disappointments than fall, as a rule, to the lot of the mortals." When the hollow comes under the Line of Fate it forebodes misfortune in many matters.

Palmistry of Knots

Fingers without knots are fingers without depth of knowledge. Knots destroy the divine beauty of the fingers; but soft, supple, smooth joints only tell a tale of idleness, unimaginativeness, unpracticality and a selfish bent of mind. Smooth-jointed people may have exalted ideals but their efforts will end in smoke.

1. From the nail downward the first knot is called the knot of philosophy. It promises a reasoned investigation into the mysteries of life.

2. The second knot is that of orderliness. It promises punctuality, exactness in office routine and business administration.

3. Where finger joins the hand is the third knot. It is a knot of domestic duty and general orderliness in the house.

Knotlessness underlies a rabid influx of ideas. It indicates inspiration unchecked by reasoned criticism. "With smooth fingers", says E. Rene, "a religious enthusiast will be carried away by devotion and may become a fanatic."

When the first knot is present but the second absent, the owner is fond of finding faults with others. When both the knots are present, the owner has an analytical and investigative mind.

Tipping the Types

In marriage and other everyday relations do not imagine that likes attract likes. In fact, quite reverse is the case. People of the same virtues and vices are often at loggerheads, because they cannot accommodate one another. "Extremes meet", says E. Rene, "and in so doing supply deficiencies of character, or support the weaker as the case may be. Mercurial people attract those of the temperament of Luna. Saturn and Apollo, being of opposite natures, are magnetically drawn to one another. Mars and Venus have a liking for each other. Jupiter, being of a social disposition, is friendly with each and all."

Palmistry recognises the fact the minds in sympathy with each other are magnetically attracted from great distances and that alone accounts for a successful marriage. Palmistry can help that process by consciously bringing such people together to make a short-cut to mutual happiness. "The only theory I advance is", says Cheiro, "that, as the press of finger on the telegraph keyboard in New York at the same moment affects the keyboard in London, so by the medium of ether, which is more subtle than electricity, are all

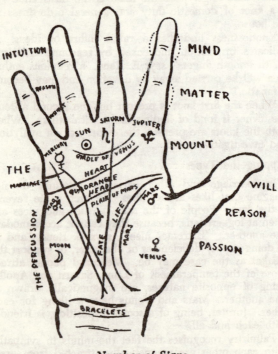

Number of Signs

persons unconsciously in touch with and in communion with one another."

Purpose of Palmistry

The purpose of Palmistry is to strengthen our virtues and weaken our vices by showing us the right road and pointing out the pitfalls along the route. It follows scientific methods to determine our future and fortune.

"It is the purpose of Palmistry", says Comte C. de Saint-Germain, "to teach you how to conquer the ancient art of divination by means of stated rules and not by intuition. These rules work accurately at all times and under all circumstances, while intuition comes and goes at its own sweet will under the influence of some momentary excitement which develops, in very rare occasions, a state of true clairvoyance, never to be fully depended upon. In the human body every element is combined to form a clear, distinct individuality: the features of the face, the irregularities of the skull, the length or shortness of limbs, the bearing, the walk, the look, the words, the gestures—everything, even to the handwriting; and above all, the members that trace the writing: the hand."

Therefore, there cannot be a greater mistake than to pass a hasty judgment on the career and character of the humblest being whose palm you are called upon to read. Everything must be carefully considered before you dare venture your opinion based on scientific study and not merely a ray of intuition. To every young student of Palmistry I recommend this principle of Cheiro:—

The greatest truth may lie in smallest things,
The greatest good in what we most despise,
The greatest light may break from darkest skies,
The greatest chord from e'en the weakest strings.

ALPHABETICALLY INDEXED

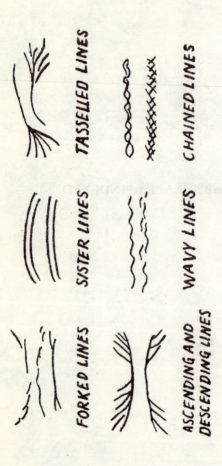

THE ISLAND | THE CIRCLE | THE TRIANGLE | THE STAR | THE SQUARE

THE GRILLE | THE CROSS | THE SPOT

A

Ability, Line of

"The Line of Apollo is really the Line of Ability If one does not have this line, it does not mean that he has no abilities. They could be shown elsewhere in the hand."

Absence of any Main Line

Absence of any Main Line, like Life, Head, Heart, Fate, etc., indicates fatality. If such a line is absent in both hands, it is a sure indication of misfortune.

Accidents

Accidents are of various kinds and these are indicated differently on the hand.

1. *Liability to accident*—a cross on the Mount of Saturn; a star in the Plain of Mars.
2. *Serious accident*—cross on the Line of Head under the Mount of Apollo or Saturn.
3. *Motor car accident*—a Line of Influence from the Line of Life to the Mount of Saturn.
4. *Accident with an animal*—a Line of Influence from the Mount of Venus to the Mount of Saturn.
5. *Accident leading to paralysis*—a black spot on the Mount of Mercury.

Actor

Qualities of an actor are shown by:

Long Line of Head.
Head Line forked at the termination.
Fingers with conical tips.
Well-developed Mount of Sun.
Palm shorter than fingers.

Fourth finger good.
Mount of Mercury strong.

Administrative Triangle

The Triangle of Brilliant Administrative Ability is indicated in the centre of the palm, below the middle finger.

Adventure

The subject is a great traveller and adventurer if the Line of Mars goes across the entire hand at its base and ends on the Mount of Moon.

Adventure, Live-Dangerously

Line of Head slightly drooping.
Large Mount of Sun.
Mounts of Mars, Jupiter and Moon predominant.
Third finger much above average.
Strong soft palm.
Palm shorter than fingers.
Spatulate finger-tips.

Advice, Need for

The merging of the Head Line and the Heart Line indicates a period when a person needs advice from others and should follow their lead until such time as the lines break out free and follow their independent courses.

Affection, Want of

If the Line of Affection is comparatively thinner than other lines in the hand, it suggests that the subject lacks in real affection. If he has many such lines, he tends to become a master flirt.

Aggressiveness

A predominance of the Mounts of Saturn and Mars is a sign of choleric temper and aggressiveness of nature.

Agriculturist

Taste for farming life is indicated by:
Broad palm.
Long finger of Saturn.
Hard stiff hand.
Strong Mount of Mars (hunting taste)
Main lines strong, others insignificant.
Mount of Saturn quite marked.
Thumb ordinary.
Long thick nails.
Spatulate finger tips.

Ague

A black spot on the first phalanx of the second finger.

Alcoholic Insanity

A black dot on the Line of Head.
Star on the Mount of the Moon.
Line of Mars very red.
Line of Mars ending in a fork.

Allahdin's Lamp

Palmistry is not for the clouds. It is a down-to-earth science. It is something which you can use everyday like your wrist watch. Hardly there is an activity of life in which Palmistry will not come readily at your command if you permit it to be the Allahdin's Lamp for you.

—*An Indian Palmist*
PRACTICAL PALMISTRY

Alternation of Events

I have also found that, as a general rule, the alternate seven years of life are somewhat alike in relation to the changes in the health of the body. For example, a child of very delicate health, when passing the end of the first seven years will also repeat the same delicacy when passing the end of the alternate seven, such as between the twentieth and twenty-first year. Such observations materially assist one in making predictions about health.

—Cheiro

Ambition

See "Successful Ambitious Career".

Ambition, Political

The Line of Fate going up to the Mount of Jupiter.

Ambition without Limit

A line from the Upper Mount of Mars to the Mount of Sun.
Mount of Sun exaggerated.
Line of Heart absent.
Head Line not joining Life Line.
Head Line crossing the hand like a bar.
Line of Life with an upward branch.
First finger abnormally long.
Exaggerated Mount of Jupiter.

Amorous Disposition

Drooping Line of Head.
Girdle of Venus very clear.
Mount of Venus rayed.
Hard and thick hands.

Anaemia

A poverty of red corpuscles in the blood, indicating a general debility. See "Bloodlessness".

Aneurism

or dilatation of an artery is indicated by:
Line of Heart broken under the Mount of Saturn.
Exaggerated Mount of the Sun.
Mount of Sun much lined.

Anger, Habitual

Unhealthy Line of Heart.
Small Mount of Venus.
Mount of Mars above normal.
Pale nails.

Animals, Affection for

Love of animals is shown by.
First phalanx of fingers below normal.
A fine and long line of Heart.
Strong Mount of Venus.
Strong Mount of Sun.

Apollo, Line of

The Line of Apollo or Sun runs up to the Mount of Apollo under the third finger. It is also known as the Line of Brilliancy, because it promises fame and name in life.

"It is one of the most thoroughly misunderstood of all the lines, and the mistaken reading of it has caused practitioners many mortifications."

—William G. Benham

The best and the most reasonable interpretation is that it indicates tendencies which, if directed along the right lines, are capable of accomplishing much. That is to say, it is a line of capability, expressive of the possible accomplishments in which the subject excels.

Apollo Line, Readings from

The Line of Apollo normally starts from the Rascette and ends on the Mount of Apollo. The following indications are easily understood:

Absence of Apollo Line—Failure in enterprises.
Normal—Brilliant intellectuality.
Long and uncrossed—Riches.
Straight and deep—Fame in art and literature.
Well-formed in both hands—Sure success in life.
Chained—Poor success.
Very broad—Shallow success.
Wavy—Lack of concentration.
Bars on the line—Rivals in profession.

Apollonian Type

A person with the Mount of Apollo predominant is called the Apollonian. He is thoroughly affectionate, healthy and hearty. A great love of beauty is his most abiding characteristic. He loves music and dance highly. His life is poetry. He makes a good stage-player. Many stage-stars are in this category. He is dominated by a colourful life and is extremely entertaining.

Apollo, Qualities of the Mount of

Normal—Happy-go-lucky dreamer, idealistic artist, fondness of excitement.

Above normal—Mad genius, over-rated talent, cupidity stifling real art.

Below normal—Artistic dreamer; gifted cleverness; contempt for culture and literature.

Apoplexy

It is a malady arresting powers of sense and motion, usually caused by effusion of blood or serum in the brain. It is shown by:

Two perpendicular lines from the Line of Heart to the Mount of the Moon.
Red scar on the Line of Heart.
Line of Liver very uneven.
Line of Liver red where it crosses the Line of Heart.
A grille or star on the Mount of the Moon.
A sprig on Mount of Jupiter.
Mount of Jupiter exaggerated.
Mount of Jupiter much lined.
Very red skin of the palm.
Plain of Mars hollow towards the Head Line.

Apparatus of a Palmist

A sheet of paper, a small wad of cotton and a pencil, in addition to the printer's ink, is all that you will need to make perfect prints. To remove the ink use a small amount of turpentine.

—*Frances Kienzle*

Architect

Aptitude for Architectural Engineering is indicated by:

A straight Line of Head.
A long finger of Saturn.
The first phalanx of fingers long.
Long straight spatulate finger of Apollo.
Strong Mount of Venus.
Mount of Sun excellent.
Mount of Mercury good.
Long second phalanx of thumb.
Long square nails.

Square-tipped fingers.
Spatulate hand.

Arm, Accident to

Wound on either arm is indicated by cross lines on the Mount of Sun.

Arms, Wounds on

Very small lines on the Mount of Sun.

Art and Science combined

See "Science and Art Combined".

Art, Failure in

See "Failure in Art".

Artistic Hand

The artists have conic hands, usually medium-sized. The palm is slightly tapering. The fingers are full at the base. They are slightly pointed at the tip or nail phalanx. They are influenced by colour, music, dance, tears and joy. They are essentially emotional.

Artist, Very Great

Extraordinary success in art is indicated by:
    The Line of Sun starting from the Line of Life.
    A branch from the Line of Head to the Mount of Sun.
    Line of Fate terminating on the Mount of Sun.
    Good Mount of Luna.
    Good space between Jupiter and Saturn fingers.
    A pointed finger of Jupiter.
    Long first phalanx of Apollo finger.
    A good straight long finger of Appollo.

Assassination

Danger of death by assassination is indicated by:
    A cross or star on the Upper Mount of Mars.
    A large cross in the centre of the Triangle.
    A star on the third phalanx of the second finger.
"A line from the Quadrangle under the Mount of Saturn cutting deep into a Girdle of Venus"

                              —*Comte C. de Saint-Germain*

Asthma

A black spot inside the Quadrangle.
Line of Liver poorly traced.
Line of Heart curving down to the Line of Head.
Narrow Quadrangle.

Astronomer

Aptitude for Astronomy is indicated by:
    Thumb above normal.
    Second phalanges of fingers unusual.
    Line of Head clear and strong.
    Mount of Saturn prominent.
    Mount of Mercury well-developed.
    Long and knotted fingers.
    Square finger-tips.
    Hard bony palm.

Astro-Palmistry

A careful examination of the various mounts, fingers, lines, stars, crosses, etc., of the palm will reveal to a clever student whether the planets in the horoscope of that person are strong and well-placed or weak and ill-placed. We have already seen that there are mainly seven mounts which represent the seven important planets out of the nine which are said to be of astrological importance. These mounts and lines certainly give a clue as to whether the planets are favourably disposed or not in the horoscope.

—*E. R. Nayanar*,
PALMISTRY AND ASTROLOGY

Audacity

Audacity of temperament is indicated by:
A very good Line of Liver.
Fine Line of Heart.
Wide Plain of Mars.
Mount of Jupiter prominent.
Upper Mount of Mars strong.
Lines of Life and Head separated at the start.
First phalanx of the thumb long.
Spatulate smooth fingers.

Author, Unimaginative

An author with knotted fingers will exhibit little imagination in the writing of his books. Histories, biographies, travels will be more within his scope than poesy or imaginative plots or picturesque descriptions.

Avarice

Avarice is indicated by:
Line of Heart terminating on the Mount of Mercury.
All mounts dried up.
Often no Line of Heart.
Line of Head crossing the palm like a bar.
Narrow Quadrangle.
Thin hard hand.
Fingers bent forward.
Fingers square-tipped.
Fingers knotted

Avoiding Mistakes, Capacity of

A whorl under the second finger.

B

Bad Teeth

A wavy Line of Liver.
A long and wavy Line of Heart.

Bankruptcy

A bad break on the Line of Fate, indicating financial ruin.
Island on the Line of Liver.
The Mount of Mercury insignificant
A poor Mount of the Sun.
The Mount of Sun covered with confused lines.
A poor Line of Sun.

Beauty, Contempt for

Poor Line of Heart.
Stiff Line of Head.
Mount of Moon insignificant.
Mount of the Moon absent.
Third finger very short.
Spatulate fingers.
Hard palm.

Benevolence

Line of Fate starting inside the Mount of Venus.
A wide Quadrangle.
A specially good Line of Heart.
The Line of Heart starting from the Mount of Jupiter
Line of Heart forked.
Mount of Jupiter good.
Mount of Venus excellent.
Soft hands.
Long nails.

Between Two Lovers

A Line from the Mount of Venus with a cross on it.

Bile and Crime

It is also a fact that the bilious types are the only ones which are really criminal, other types doing bad things under a stress of some exciting cause. Bad types of Saturnians and Mercurians prefer the criminal way of doing things to the honest one.

—*William G. Benham*

Bilious Headache

Small line cutting through the Hepatica.

Biliousness

Mount of Mercury much lined
Wavy Line of Liver.
Cold clammy skin.
Yellow-hued palm.

Blackmailer

A blackmailer is indicated by:
A prong of the Head Line running into the Mount of the Moon.
Mount of Mercury predominant and crossed.
Mounts of Jupiter and Sun excessive.
Pointed crooked fingers.
Thin long hands.

Blackmarketing

Business dishonesty, deceit, treachery and blackmarketing are indicated by an exaggerated Mount of Mercury.

Bladder Trouble

Mount of the Moon much lined.

Mount of Moon exaggerated.

Blindness

A star in the Triangle closer to the Line of Liver.
Circle on the Line of Life.
Cross on the Line of Liver.
Circle on the Line of Heart.
Cross on the Line of Head.

Blood, Bad Circulation of

Bluish nails.
A very pale Line of Heart.

Blood, Good Circulation of

Good circulation of Blood is indicated by large moons on the nails.

Bloodlessness

A very pale palm.
Mount of Moon exaggerated.
Mount of Moon much lined.
Short and pale nails.
Life Line pale and dim.

Blood Troubles

Different kinds of blood troubles are indicated as follows:—

Low Blood Pressure—Mount of Saturn is exaggerated or much lined.

Defective Circulation of Blood—White spots on the nails; Heart Line broken under the Mount of Saturn.

Blood poisoning—Black or bluish spots on nails.

Excessive flow of blood to the head—Exaggerated or much lined Mount of Mars.

Bohemianism

The unconventional ways of the Bohemian are shown by:

>Mount of Moon much developed.
>Mount of Venus exaggerated.
>First finger abnormally short.
>Very small hands.
>Soft palm.
>First phalanges flexible.
>The thumb thrown back.

Bracelets

The Bracelets are three lines nearest to the palm. These are also called the Rascette.

One clearly-marked and unbroken bracelet indicates a life of twenty-three to twenty-eight years.

Two unbroken bracelets denote a life of forty-six to fifty-six years.

Three unbroken bracelets hold out a promise of sixty-nine to eighty-six years.

Brahamcharya

or chastity inspired by religious fervour is indicated by:

>The Mounts quite insignificant.
>A very smooth thin hand.
>A cross on the first phalanx of the third finger.
>A fine pointed first finger.

Brain Fever

>Line of Head quite close to the Line of Life.
>Many bars cutting the Line of Life.
>Deep Line of Liver.
>Liver Line ending at the Line of Head.

Brain Trouble

A Line from the Mount of Venus ending on the Line of Head.
The Line of Liver joined to the Line of Head.
Line of Head starred or crossed.
Mount of Moon starred or much rayed.
Line of Head crossed by a deep bar.
Line of Head badly broken.
Line of Head sloping exaggeratedly.
Line of Life forked at the start.
Line of Head pale and wide.
Black spots on the Line of Head.
A break on the Line of Head.
A wavy Line of Head inclining towards a wavy Line of Liver.
Plain of Mars hollow towards the Head Line.
An Influence Line from the Mount of Venus cutting the Line of Head.
A star on the Line of Head at the end of a Line of Influence.

Breaks in the Lines

A break in any line shows failure of the line.

The importance of breaks as a defect is measured by their width. The wider the break, the more serious is the consequence.

On a deep strong line, the impact of the break is slight. On a shallow and chained line the damage is intense.

Breaks caused through illness or accidents are great impediments to health. A series of breaks handicap the subject and render him constitutionally weak. He lacks in vitality.

If the line grows strong after the break, it is an indication that the subject faces the handicap manfully.

If the break is followed by an island, it shows a continuity of delicacy after the mishap.

Squares and sister lines repair the expected damage caused by a break in the line.

Breast, Wounds on

Very small lines on the Mount of Mercury indicate wounds on the breast.

Another indication is capillary cross lines on the Mount of Saturn.

Bright's Disease

Bright's Disease is indicated by small white dents on the Line of Head near the Mount of Mars.

Brilliant Career

The Line of Sun starting from the foot of the Line of Life.

A line from the Line of Head terminating in a star on the Mount of Jupiter.

Brilliant Intellect

When the first phalanx of the thumb is "wasp-shaped, with centre slightly concave", it shows a brilliant intellect. The person is quick, sharp and deep.

Bronchitis

Cross lines from Percussion into the Upper Mount of Mars.

Upper Mount of Mars much lined.

Brute Animality

Instincts verging on brute animality are indicated by:
  A cross in the middle of the Triangle.
  Lines of Head and Heart short.
  Mount of Mars exaggerated.
  Mount of Venus well-developed.
  First phalanx of the thumb clubbed.

Short smooth fingers.
Characterless tips.
Much hair on the hands
Rough and red skin.
Thick clawed nails overrun by flesh.
Thick, very hard hands.

Bully

A tightly-clenched fist is typical of the bully and the reasonless fighter.

Burglar

The mind of the burglar is revealed by:
- A cross in the Triangle
- A star or grille on the Mount of Mercury.
- A star or grille on the Upper Mount of Mars.
- Lines of Life, Head and Heart, short and red.
- Mount of Moon exaggerated.
- Mounts of Mars and Venus abnormal.
- Clubbed first phalanx of thumb
- Smooth short fingers.
- Heavy, thick elementary hand.

Business, Aptitude for

- Fair Line of Fate.
- Line of Head well and deep.
- The Mount of Sun excellent.
- Line of Liver good.
- Branches from the Line of Head to the Mount of Mercury.
- Mount of Mercury most prominent.
- Fourth finger above average length.
- Good Line of Head.
- Strong first phalanx of the thumb.
- Second knot marked with square tips.
- Fingers longer than palm.

Business Man, Successful

One of the best combinations of a successful business man is the hand with both Jupiterian and Mercurian Mount developments. Here we have the ambition of the Jupiter backed by the shrewdness of the Mercurian.

—*Rita Van Alen*

Business Success

The Line of Head forked with one prong going to the Mount of Mercury.

A line rising from the base of the palm and going up to the Mount of Mercury.

A branch from the Line of Fate reaching the Mount of Mercury.

A good Mount of Mercury on both hands.

C

Cæsar, Julius

It is related by Josephius, the historian, that Julius Cæsar was so much well versed in Palmistry that "one day a so-called son of Herod had audience with him, and he at once detected the impostor because his hand was destitute of all marks of royalty"

Card Sharper

A quick-witted thug is called a card-sharper. He is indicated by:
> Lower part of the Mount of Moon high.
> The Mount of Mercury predominant.
> The Mount of Mercury crossed or starred.
> Long thin fingers often crooked.

Career, Change of

> The Line of Life forked at its termination.
> A cross on the wrist.

Catarrh

Catarrh or inflammation of mucous membrane is indicated by the Mount of Moon being excessively full towards the top.

Caution, Extreme

Hands clasped behind the back show that the subject is extremely cautious in his approach to life.

Celibacy

> A cross on the first phalanx of the second finger.
> A Line of Marriage turned up at the termination.

Chains, Signs from

On the Head Line—bronchial and throat troubles.
On the Heart Line—Weakness of organs.
On the Life Line—Delicacy in childhood.
Encircling second joint of thumb—Argumentative disposition.

Change of Lines

The lines of the hand change only under the influence of the mind, the will, the emotions and particularly under the deep-reaching influence of the disease.

—*Alice Denton Jennings*

Cheirognomy and Cheiromancy

The study of the hand is divided into two sections—the twin sciences of Cheirognomy and Cheiromancy. The first-mentioned deals with the shape of the hands and fingers, and the latter with the lines and markings of the palm.

—*Cheiro's* GUIDE TO THE HAND

Chemistry, Success in

Success in Chemistry is shown by short vertical lines on the Mount of Mercury.

Childbearing Difficulties

First bracelet of the Rascette convex in shape.
An Influence Line from the Mount of Venus to the Mount of Saturn.
The Line of Life too close to the second phalanx of the thumb.

Childlessness

Childlessness is indicated by a star on the Line of Liver.

Children

Children are indicated by short lines at the root of the fourth finger.

Children, Gender of

Read the number of lines off the Heart Line and then select the strongest vertical lines on the Affection Line and read the straight deep ones as boys and the slanted deep ones as girls.

—Frances Kienzle

Circle

A Circle is a very unusual sign. Its value must be interpreted according to the circumstances.

Circle on fingers.

People who have the circle formation on their fingertips are always eager to finish what they start.

Circles, Signs from

On the Mounts a circle shows success.
On the lines a circle denotes misfortune.

Clairvoyance

A good many minor cross lines.
The Mount of Moon prominent.
The Mount of Saturn rayed.
A soft hand.
Short smooth fingers.
A small thumb.
A drooping Line of Head.
A poor Line of Heart.
A clear Line of Intuition.
A Line of Liver islanded at the start.

Closed Fist

Closed fist is a sign of great determination. It shows the shutting in of the vital energy. A clenched fist indicates the final making of the mind.

Clubbed Thumb

The first phalanx of the "Clubbed Thumb" is thick and rounded, or broad and thick, with a nail short and very coarse in texture. It is called the "Murderer's Thumb" owing to thickness, coarseness, and brutal obstinacy. It shows a coarse degree of a good quality, terrific obstinacy and is coupled with a violent temper.

Coarseness

Heavy limp hands, belonging as if to a dead person, are an indication of coarseness and denseness of mind and body

Colour of Hand

"A very white hand indicates a poor quality of blood and a superabundance of lymph; that a yellowish tint is evidence of liver trouble of a more or less serious nature; that a red hand indicates a superabundance of blood, and a very red hand a tendency to apoplexy."

Colour of Lines, Indications from

Rosy lines—Health and optimism.
Red lines—Violent disposition.
Yellow lines—Sad temperament.
Pale lines—Deceitful nature.

Colour of the Palm

Pale—Selfish and unsympathetic.
Yellowish—Morbid, melancholy, morose.
Delicate pink—Bright and hopeful.
Red—Robust and passionate.

Combativeness

A large cross in the Triangle.
Lines redder than usual.
Upper Mount of Mars prominent.
Plenty of hair.
Broad, short nails.
Square palm.
Short smooth fingers.
Finger-tips spatulate.

Commercial Artist

Art and money-making are united if the person has:
Mount of Mercury equal to the Mount of Sun.
A straight line of Head on a Spatulate Hand.
A drooping Line of Head on a Square Hand.
Line of Sun ending on the Mount of Mercury.
Square-tipped fingers.

Commercialization of Art

A whorl between the third and fourth finger gives a person the capacity to commercialize his artistic qualities

Compass of Hand

A Line of Head is like the needle of the compass, without a true knowledge of which it is impossible to grasp the direction of the object. I have seen more mistakes caused by lack of grasp of this point than by anything else.

—*Cheiro*

Composer of Music

A good composer of music is indicated by:
Strong Mount of Mercury.

Square finger-tips.
Mount of Moon well-developed.

Concentration, Lack of

Cross lines on the Mount of Sun.
Poor, drooping Line of Head.
The Mounts of Moon and Sun exaggerated.
Mounts of Jupiter, Mars and Mercury insignificant.
Short smooth fingers.
Soft palm.
A weak short thumb.

Concentration, Power of

Mount of Moon insignificant.
Line of Head long and straight.
Mounts well-developed.
Long knotted fingers.
Strong long thumb.

Confused Lines

Confused lines show a mental confusion and a confused existence. A hand covered with a network of lines betrays a disordered planless life.

Congenital Potentialities

The right hand shows whether the subject is progressing or retrograding by comparing with the left hand which invariably denotes congenital potentialities in case of males. The process is reversed in case of females.

Conquests of Love

White spots on the Line of Heart.

Constancy

Constancy is indicated by:
Few worry lines.

Mount of Moon very small
Mount of Venus not very strong.
A long straight Line of Head.
Line of Heart forked into the Mount of Jupiter.
Strong first phalanx of the thumb.
Dominant Lower Mount of Mars.

Constitutional Brain Trouble

Absence of the Line of Head.
Island at the starting point of the Line of Head.

Constitution, Strong

Excellent Line of Liver.
The Mounts clear and firm.
No worry lines.
Life, Head and Heart lines clear and strong.
Palm thick and elastic.
Nails perfect.
Pink and mottled skin.

Constitution, Weak

Very poor Line of Liver.
Downward branches on the Line of Life.
Line of Life chained.
Nails long, thin and brittle.
Hand thin and narrow.

Consumption, Tendency to

Islands on the Line of Head.
Islands on the Line of Liver.
Mount of Jupiter exaggerated.
Mount of Jupiter much lined.
Nails long, thin, brittle, convex and fluted.
Very thin palm.
Long knotty fingers.

Convent Career

Grille on the Mount of Jupiter.
Square on the Mount of Venus.

Conventionality, Excessive

Narrow Quadrangle.
Line of Heart curving towards the Line of Head.
Lines of Life and Head connected for quite a while.
First phalanx of thumb stiff and long.
Fingers stiff and bent forward.
Hair on two lower phalanges of fingers.

Coquetry

An exaggerated Mount of Mars.
A chained Line of Heart.

Corruptibility

Short fragmentary Line of Head.
Line of Heart wavy or starred.
Crooked fingers.
Strong Girdle of Venus.

Courage

The palm firm.
Fingers unusually long.
Mounts of Venus and Jupiter fine.
Lines deep and red.
Line of Head straight and clear.
The first phalanx of the thumb above normal.
A long Line of Heart.
Line of Heart starting from the Mount of Jupiter.
Mounts large and firm.
The Plain of Mars wide.

Cowardice

The triangle small and formed of lines much curved inwards.

The Mounts of Moon, Mercury and Saturn exaggerated or badly rayed.
Mounts of Mars, Jupiter and Venus insignificant.
Fingers bent forward.
Nails long, thin and narrow.
Hand thick and flabby.
Hands without any hair.

Crank, The Qualities of

Hand spatulate.
Sloping Line of Head.
Sudden curve of the Line of Head on the Mount of Luna

Criminal Propensities

The Line of Head leaves its proper place on the hand and rises and takes possession of the Line of Heart, and sometimes even passes beyond it. Whether such people murder one or twenty is not the question. The point is that they have abnormal tendencies for crime; they stop at nothing in the accomplishment of their purpose, and under the slightest provocation or temptation they must and will gratify these strange and terrible propensities.

—*Cheiro*

Criminal Qualities

The Saturnian and the Mercurian create most of the criminals of the world. Both of them are instinctively hostile to mankind, the former because of his moody manners, the latter because of his money-mindedness. They cannot be reformed, because the poison of callousness is in their blood. This psychological poison perverts everything and converts it into evil.

Critical Faculty

Short well-formed nails are indicative of great critical faculty. Such people love arguments. Other indications are:

    Cross in the Plain of Mars.
    Mount of Mercury predominant.
    Second phalanges of all fingers above normal.
    Fingers with strong first knot.
    Soft palm.
    Short nails.

Critical Illness

"It is said that in critical illness, when the patient ceases to fight for life, the thumb turns in towards the palm in complete apathy."

Critical Intellect

An aptitude for details and an analytical mind is indicated by:

    Second phalanges above normal size.
    Large hands.
    Long knotty fingers.
    Strong thumb knot.
    Second phalanx of the thumb strong.

Cross

A cross is an obstacle in life. It also indicates poor health.

Cross-Bar

These are horizontal lines and are not a good sign.

Cross of Mental Suffering

The Cross of Mental Suffering is found at the base between the first and the second fingers. It denotes a deep suffering due to one's beliefs. This cross was found on the hand of the famous Russian writer and reformer, Count Léo Tolstoy.

Crosses, Signs from

Crosses must be independent of lines, not formed partly by them. An ill-made uneven cross is a bad sign, but if well-formed and clear, it is not unfavourable.

—*E. Rene*

Crosses give the following indications:—
  On the Triangle—change in life.
  On the Quadrangle—interest in occult.
  On the Mount of Jupiter—happy marriage.
  On the Mount of Saturn—ill health.
  On the Mount of Apollo—financial trouble.
  On the Mount of Mercury—taking undue advantage.
  On the Mount of Mars (under Mercury)—stealing.
  On the Mount of Mars (under Jupiter)—tendency to commit suicid
  On the Mouht of Luna—danger in water.
  On the Mount of Venus—unhappy love affair.
  On the Line of Apollo—money by chance, a windfall.
  On the Hepatica—illness
  On the Life Line—serious illness.
  On the Line of Heart—love trouble.
  On the Line of Head—injury to head.
  On the Line of Fate—change for the worse.

Cruelty, Instinctive

Very narrow Quadrangle.
Very bad Line of Liver.
Drooping Line of Head.
Mounts of Mercury and Sun exaggerated or badly formed.
Mounts of Mars surprisingly insignificant.
Small palm.
Very long thin fingers.

Very small hands.
Hairy hands in women.

Cunning

When the nails are short, square and pale, they indicate a person given to falsehood and cunning.

Curiosity

Line of Head separated from the Line of Life at the start.
Many worry lines.
Mounts of Sun, Mercury and Moon predominant.
Short nails.
Straggling flexible fingers "showing light between".

D

Danger Signal

Worst type of danger is indicated if the line turns back after the break, forms some sort of a hook, and returns towards the source. It shows a great disaster, even a catastrophe. But if it is joined by a sister line or a square, the great danger is avoided.

Deafness

Deafness is indicated by:
Exaggerated Mount of Saturn.
Mount of Saturn much rayed.
Bulging Mount of Venus.
Dots on the Line of Head.
Island under the Mount of Saturn.

Death by Execution

Line of Head broken under the Mount of Saturn.
Cross in the Plain of Mars.
Star on the second finger.
Line of Life terminating abruptly, showing date of execution.

Death, Early

The Lines of Head and Heart stopping short before reaching the Line of Fate.
A short Line of Life in both hands.
The Line of Head wavy.

Death in War

Fine Mount of Jupiter.
Plain of Mars excellent.
Star on the Upper Mount of Mars.

A line from the Upper Mount of Mars to the Mount of Saturn.

Death, Prediction of

In no case, therefore, should absolute statements be made that death will come at a given time, for, while you may see great danger, will-power will be strong enough to wrest life from death.

—*William G. Benham*

Death Signals

1. When the Life Line stops suddenly, a sudden death is indicated.
2. Cuts, spots, breaks, or cracks on the Line of Life indicate grave danger to health.
3. Death is a certainty when there are grave dangers in the Life Line as well as the Head and Heart Lines.
4. Lines from the Mount of Saturn cutting Life Line indicate death from accident or operation.
5. Cross bars or vertical lines on the Life Line indicate danger of death.
6. A line parallel to a break shows safety from grave danger to death.

Death, Sudden and Violent

Grille on the Upper Mount of Mars.
Cross on the middle of the Line of Head.
One short downward line on the joints of all the fingers.
Lines of Life, Head, and Heart joined at the start in both hands.
Line of Life ending in a deep scar.

Deceitful Disposition

Drooping Line of Head.
Line of Head widely forked.
Mount of Moon predominant.

Cross lines on the Mount of Mercury.
Fourth finger long and crooked.
Long, thin fingers.
Short and pale nails.

Definition

It is the purpose of Palmistry to teach you how to conquer the ancient art by means of stated rules and not by intuition.

—Comte C de Saint-Germain
THE STUDY OF PALMISTRY

Details, Love of

No Mount of the Moon.
Long and straight Line of Head.
Mounts of Jupiter and Mercury dominant.
Long second phalanx of the thumb.
Fingers long and knotted.

Detective Method

I endeavour to study every phase of thought that can throw light on human life; consequently the very ridges of the skin, the hair found on the hands, all are used, as a detective would use a clue to accumulate evidence.

—Cheiro

Devoted Love

An overflowing devotion of affection is indicated:
    Large thumb with firm hands.
    A double Line of Love.

Diabetes

Cross on the Mount of the Moon.
Confused lines at the bottom of the Mount of the Moon.

Dimensions of Lines

On the whole, long lines are better than short lines. A good line is long and deep but not too wide.

Every line must be considered very carefully, because as Michelet said, "The convulsions of the brain are written in the hands."

The deeper the line, the more profound is the quality indicated by it.

"A line", says Comte de Saint-Germain, "must not be spread too much in its course, or it loses its qualities as a channel for the transmission of the nervous fluid whatever name we please to give it. Like a river that runs over its banks, it ceases to be useful as a carrier and its shallowness destroys its efficiency."

Diphtheria

Spots on the Line of Head under the Mount of Jupiter.

Diplomat, Successful

A successful career as a diplomat is indicated by a pointed fourth finger with a triangle on the Mount of Mercury.

Disappointment in Ambition

Downward branches from the Lines of Life, Fate and Sun.

Cross lines on the Mounts of Mercury and Sun.

The Line of Life entering deep into the Mount of Jupiter and getting barred or crossed.

Disappointment in Love

Influence lines from the Line of Life cutting the Line of Heart.

Influence lines from the Mount of Venus cutting the Line of Heart.

Branches from the Line of Fate cutting the Line of Heart.

Many downward branches on the Line of Heart.
The Line of Heart barred, crossed, or starred at the start.

Disappointments, Life full of

The Line of Life throwing small branches towards the Rascette.

Discontent, Habitual

The Mount of Moon predominant.
The Mount of Moon much rayed.
Many worry lines.
Poor Line of Life.
Line of Heart wretched.
Line of Liver bad.
First phalanx of the thumb small.
Short smooth fingers.
A thin palm.

Discoveries, New

White spots on the Line of Head,

Disease, Incurable

A cross cut by the downward branch from the Line of Life.
A star on the Mount of Saturn.

Disposition, Feverish

A feverish disposition is indicated by dark spots on the Line of Head.

Divisions of Hand

According to Cheiro the hand is divided into two parts or hemispheres:—The Upper Hemisphere, containing the fingers, and Mounts of Jupiter, Saturn, Sun, Mercury, and Mars, representing mind; and the Lower

Hemisphere, containing the base of the hand, representing matter. They represent spiritual and material qualities respectively.

Divorce

A future divorce is indicated by the following signs on the hand of the subject:—

1. A line of influence from the Mount of Venus reaching Life Line and ending in a fork.
2. Line of influence from Mount of Venus cutting an upward branch of the Line of Life.
3. Line of influence from the Mount of Venus cutting the Line of Marriage.
4. Line of Marriage starting with a fork.
5. Line of Marriage terminating with a fork.

Dogged Determination

People with stiff-jointed thumbs have dogged determination. They are practical but cautious and secretive.

Domestic Disease

A Line of Influence terminating in a black dot on the Line of Heart indicates domestic worries causing a serious heart disease.

Domestic Trouble

Plain of Mars hollow.
Line of Influence from the Mount of Venus cutting Main Lines.
Line of Influence from Life Line cutting Main Lines.

Domineering Personality

Short and wide nails indicate a pugnacious and domineering person.

Don't-Marry Line

When the Line of Marriage is full of little islands, or linked by the loops of a chain, the subject should be warned not to marry at any time, as such union will be full of the greatest unhappiness and continual separation.

Dot

Dots on the line point out defects. Small dots appear after illness. Big permanent dots indicate a serious defect.

Dots, Signs from

On the Line of Life—typhus.
On the Mounts—wounds.
On the Head Line—deafness.
On the Heart Line—Heart trouble.

Double Crossing

Two Lines of Influence meeting in a star on the Line of Fate indicate two simultaneous love affairs ruining each other.

Double Line of Heart

A Double Line of Heart indicates capacity for deep abiding affection. It will end in sorrow like Gray's Elegy.

Dramatic Art

The Line of Extraordinary Dramatic Expression rises from the side of the hand in the vicinity of the Mount of Luna towards the base of the middle finger. It indicates brilliant histrionic genius. It indicates an extraordinary imagination which wipes out consciousness of self in the re-creation of dramatic character.

Dramatic Genius

Aptitude for dramatic profession is indicated by:
The Lines of Life and Head separated at the start.
The Line of Head with a fork at the end.
High Mounts of Jupiter, Sun and Mercury.
Good first phalanx of the thumb.
Square fingers with no knots.

Dreamer

A habitual dreamer has the following indications:—
A cross near the Line of the Sun.
Line of Intuition islanded.
Very drooping Line of Head.
Mounts of Moon, Venus and Saturn prominent.
Thin elongated palm.
Long, slender-pointed fingers.

Dropsy

A star on the Mount of the Moon indicates dropsy.

Drowning, Danger from

Lines arising from inside the Rascette and ending in a star on the Mount of the Moon.
Wavy cross lines on the first phalanges of all fingers.
An angle or star on the Mount of the Moon.
A star on a voyage line from the Percussion.

Drunkenness

An upward line from the Triangle ending on the Mount of the Moon.

A branch from the Mount of Venus ending in a star on the Mount of the Moon.

An Influence Line from the Line of Life ending on the Mount of the Moon.

E

Economy

A very strong and straight Line of Head.
The first finger relatively longer than the rest.

Effeminacy

The Mounts of Moon and Venus predominant.
Mounts of Mars, Jupiter and Mercury absent.
Hands thin, pale and soft.
Hands without any hair.

Egotism, Boundless

Grille on the Mount of Jupiter.
Line of Head crossing the hand like a bar.
Often no Line of Heart.
Lines stiff and too highly coloured.
Mounts of Jupiter and Sun exaggerated.
Large first phalanx of the thumb.

Electric Life-Current

Attempts to solve the Lines in the hands have for ages presented the stumbling block which has baffled both authors and practitioners alike. The working hypothesis of an electric life-current I introduced in the original publication in 1900: today it is a fact, proved by the discoveries of scientific men that each cell is an electric dynamo, and energy generated by thought has been recorded on graphs.

—*William G. Benham*

Elementary Hand

An Elementary Hand is characterized by stiff heavy fingers. It has a short clumsy thumb. It has an extremely thick, hard palm. It is often of the clubbed type. These hands undertake unskilled manual labour. To these hands belongs war, where no personal prowess and no intelligent leadership is needed.

"And yet Elementary Hands", says Comte C. de Saint-Germain, "are almost invariably more accessible to the charms of poetry or simple music than those of science. It was to the lyrical measure of Orpheus and to harmonies of the flute of Apollo, that in the Greek world the first communities of men were formed, and the first towns were built."

Eloquence

Line of Head long, forked and sloping.
Line of Heart excellent.
Mount of Venus in good shape.
Fine Mounts of Jupiter and Sun.
Lines of Life and Head separated at the start.

Embezzler

Thin soft hand.
Fingers long and knotty.
Mounts of Jupiter and Sun exaggerated.
Widely forked Line of Head.
Mount of Mercury predominant.
Star or grille on the Mount of Mercury.
Third finger above normal in length.
Fourth finger crooked.

Emotions and Mounts

It has been observed that all with the Mounts, apparent or prominent, are swayed by their feelings and emotions rather than the people who have flat palms and undeveloped Mounts.

—Cheiro

Energetic Personality

Line of Head separated from the Line of Life.
Long Line of Head.
Mounts of Mars and Jupiter predominant
First phalanx of thumb strong.
Short nails.
Hand thick and hard.
Hands slightly hairy.

Engagement, Broken

Line of Heart broken.
Line of Heart broken under the Mount of Saturn—
Engagement broken by circumstances.
Heart Line broken under the Mount of Sun—
Caprice broke engagement.
Heart Line broken under the Mount of Mercury—
Love of money was the main cause.

Engineer's Hand

Broad palm.
Flat Mounts.
Spatulate fingers.
Straight Line of Head.
Mounts of Mars large and fine.
Scientific markings on the Mount of Mercury.
Mount of Saturn predominant.
Long knotty fingers.

Envy

A ring on the Mount of Sun.
Cross lines on the third phalanx of the third finger.
Poor fragmentary Line of Sun.
Mount of Sun exaggerated.
Mount of Sun much lined.

Epilepsy

Short nails with a much broken Line of Head.

Events Determining Signs

Nature's books are within the reach of all, and once we have the key, much may be learned by personal observation, by listening to tales of woe, adventure, sickness, or other experiences, and after examining the hands of the narrator. With a knowledge of how and where to search, we may trace past events, and not infrequently discover the probable consequences or sequel to such a story.

—*E. Rene*
HANDS AND HOW TO READ THEM

Excitement, Temporary

When a person is toying with his buttons, handkerchief, etc., it shows a temporary nervous excitement.

Extravagance

Line of Fate stopping early.
Line of Sun dim or absent.
Mount of Sun poor.
Sloping Line of Head.
Line of Life separated from the Line of Head at the commencement.
Fingers flexible.
Thumb set very low.
First phalanx of the thumb thrown backwards.

Eye Trouble

A circle on the Line of Heart under the Mount of the Sun.
Broken Line of Head under the Mount of Saturn or Sun.

Line of Influence from the Mount of Venus ending in a black dot or star.
Mount of Sun exaggerated or much lined.
Ill-formed circle on the Mount of Sun.
Poor Line of Sun.
White dot on Line of Life.

F

Faculty of Investigation

When the third phalanges of fingers are waist-like, these indicate a spirit of inquiry.

"If the phalanx is waist-like", says William G. Benham, "the subject is only a slight eater, and his brain, instead of being clogged and heavy, has force to expand, and does it through the faculty of investigation. This waist-like indication, so estimated, is very accurate in its results, and may be used freely as showing little care for money, an absence of gluttony, and the enquiring, even curious, mind."

THE LAWS OF SCIENTIFIC HAND-READING

Failure Due to Women

The Ring of Venus well-formed but cut by a deep bar under the Mount of Sun.

Failure in Art

Poor Mount of Sun.
Small Mount of Venus.
Line of Sun broken.
Poor Line of Head.
First phalanx of the thumb small.
Mount of Jupiter exaggerated.

Fainting Fits

The Line of Head rising towards the Line of Heart.
The Line of Liver rising from the Line of Life.
The Line of Heart curving to the Line of Head.
Line of Heart chained.
Line of Liver connected with the Line of Life at the start.

Faithfulness

Rosy nails show firmness, loyalty and constancy of purpose.

Fame

A clearly marked Line of Sun.
A star on the Mount of Jupiter

Fame and Name

A career of great distinction is indicated by:
  Fine Mount of Moon (for art and intellect).
  Mounts of Moon and Saturn missing (for politics and business).
  Lines of Head and Heart normal and long.
  Sister lines on the Mount of Sun.
  Line of Liver perfect.
  Star on the Mount of Jupiter.
  Star at the end of the Line of Sun
  Line of Fate from Rascette to the Mount of Jupiter, Sun or Saturn.

Fame, Ladder of

Study and development are one-half the ladder of fame. Genius sits on the rungs to dream; Study works and rises rung by rung; it is the earthworms alone who, dazzled by the heights above them, confound the two, and often crown Study and call it Genius.

—*Cheiro*

Family Affection

Family affection is indicated by the fingers and the palm of even size with the Mount of Jupiter well-deyeloped.

Family Responsibility

A bulge upwards on the Head Line indicates family responsibility, invalids, widows, etc.

Famous People, Hands of

According to Rita Van Alen, President Eisenhower has "dependable and conservative hands". General MacArthur has "conscientious hands". Stalin had "secretive hands" by the very way he unconsciously held them. "Winston Churchill's thumbs reveal a personally generous side of his nature". His familiar "Thumb up" so well-known to the world, helped to stiffen the backbone of a war-worn nation.

Fanaticism

Long, thin, smooth fingers.

Branch from the Line of Head to the Mount of Jupiter.

Second finger with exaggerated first phalanx.

"With smooth fingers a religious enthusiast will be carried away by devotion, and may become a fanatic."

—*E. Rene*

Fatal Influence of Women

A crescent on the Mount of Moon indicates a fatal influence of women.

Fatalism

There is no fatalism about Palmistry. There is nothing inevitable about the signs in the palm. Both lines and events are changeable. Cheiro sums it up as follows: "There is a tendency in the subject's nature which will produce certain results, unless the tendency is checked."

Fatal Love Affair

Two lines joining the Line of Fate low down, one rising from the Mount of Venus and the other from the Mount of Moon.

Fatalistic, Palmistry is not

There is no greater truth than that we are indeed free agents, planned for a pre-arranged destiny but always able to change it if we determinedly desire to do so. There is indeed no such thing as absolute fatalism.

—*William G. Benham*

Fate and Fatality

The Line of Fate rises at the base of the hand and goes upward towards the fingers. It receives the current of personal magnetism and is also called the Line of Saturn.

"Upon first thought it may not be apparent why fatality, good or bad, has been ascribed to this line, but the claim is justified in various ways."

—*Benham*

Fate Line, Absence of

People without any sign of a Line of Fate are often very successful, but they lead more or less a vegetable kind of existence.

—*Cheiro*

Fate Line, Readings from

The Line of Fate starts from the Rascette, near the wrist, and goes straight up to the Mount of Saturn.
1. Absence of line—unprofitable existence.
2. Rising from the Heart Line—success in old age.

3. Unusually deep—perseverance against heavy odds.
4. Chained—difficulties.
5. Wavy—ups and downs.
6. Irregular—irritability.
7. Terminating at Head Line—bad luck through misjudgment.
8. Terminating at Heart Line—failure through despondency.
9. Terminating at the Mount of Jupiter—success in everything.
10. Reaching the Mount of Sun—literary success.
11. Break—misfortune.
12. Bars—obstacles.
13. Cross—violent death.
14. Island—gift of occult.
15. Square—protection from financial loss.

Fault-Finding

The habit of finding faults with others is indicated by:

    Line of Heart poor.
    Mount of Venus small.
    Mounts of Mars exaggerated.
    Poor Line of Liver.
    Narrow Quadrangle.
    Two stars near the thumb nails.
    Short nails.
    Long knotty fingers.
    Fingers spatulate.

Female Troubles

Line of Life turning towards the Mount of Moon.
Plain of Mars hollow towards the Mount of Moon.
Mount of Moon exaggerated or much lined.
Cross on the Mount of Moon.

Fickle Fancy

When the Line of Head rises from inside the Mount of Mars, it makes a person fretful, of worrying nature, inconstant in thought and action. "The shifting sands of the sea are more steadfast than are the ideas of such an individual."

Financial Failure

A very hollow palm.
A cross on the Mount of Mercury.

Financial Instability

Island on the Line of Fate.
Island on the Line of Liver.
Star or island on the Line of Sun.
Hollow Plain of Mars.
Breaks or bars on the Line of Sun.

Financial Trouble and Losses

Island on the Line of Liver.
Cross on the Mount of Mercury.
A line from the Mount of Mercury cutting the Line of Heart.
Lines of influence from the Mount of Venus cutting the Line of Sun.
Downward branches on the Line of Fate.
Downward branches on the Line of Sun.
Breaks, crosses and stars on lines of Fate and Sun.

Finger-joints, Well-formed

Men with these developed joints have an almost feminine instinct in matters of dress—they class and blend colours well, and nothing will irritate them more than to accompany a woman the colours of whose costume do not harmonize.

—*Cheiro*

Fingers, General Qualities of

Set evenly on a line—success.
Set close together—inquisitiveness.
Set very close—meanness.
Equally spaced—unconventionality.
Keeping together—social difficulties.
Bent forward—meanness.
Flexible fingers—financial irresponsibility
Stiff—practical nature.
Bent backwards—cheerfulness.

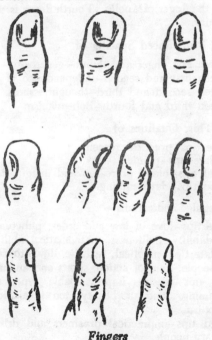

Fingers

Finger Lines, Indications from

Triangle—tendency to sickness.
Wavy cross lines—danger ahead.
Vertical lines—sudden death.
Little balls—extreme sensitiveness.

Fingers, Names of

Fingers are named after the mounts under them. First finger is called the finger of Jupiter. The second finger is known as the finger of Saturn. The third finger is the finger of Apollo. Fourth finger is the finger of Mercury.

Fingers, Pronounced Spacing of

Between first finger and thumb—generosity.
Between first and second—independence of thought.
Between second and third—thoughtlessness.
Between third and fourth—Bohemianism.

Finger Tips, Qualities of

Square tips—practical reason.
Spatulate tips—planless work.
Conical tips—blend of reason and imagination.
Pointed tips—daydreaming.

More detailed indications:—

Square tips—love of law and order; punctuality, dependability, politeness, mathematical ability.
Spatulate tips—practical, realistic, down-to-earth type of people, fond of action, sports and animals.
Conic tips—artistic, impressionable type, talented, dreaming, fond of beauty, too idealistic to be practical.
Pointed tips—impractical dreamers and drifters, visionary people.

First Finger, Abnormal

When the first finger is abnormal, namely, as long as the second finger, it indicates great pride of disposition, a desire for power, 'one man, one world' creed. Napoleon was a striking example of this rule; on his hand the first finger was abnormal, it being fully equal to the second.

—*Cheiro*

First Finger, Qualities of

Crooked—want of honour.
Too long—tyranny.
Too short—escapism.
Fair size—active disposition.
Low-set—awkwardness in social matters
Leaning towards the thumb—deep desire for independence.
Leaning towards the second finger—great pride.
Longer than the second—domineering instinct.
Equal to the second—love of power.
Shorter than the second—reticent in everything.
Longer than the third—unhealthy ambition
Equal to the third—great desire for fame and riches.
Much shorter than the third—humdrum existence.

Flexibility

Flexibility of the hand indicates flexibility of the mind. When the hand is flexible, the mind can see "round the corners of things". When the hand is stiff, the mind is cautious, immobile, narrow and stingy. It lacks adaptability. Such a person is shy of new ideas and new ventures.

Flirtation

Island on the Line of Heart.
A fork in the Line of Marriage.

The Mount of Venus exaggerated.
A chained Line of Head.

Forger

No Mount of Jupiter.
Line of Head straight and widely forked.
Mount of Moon heavy.
Star on the Mount of Mercury.
Long, slender, crooked fingers.
Mount of Mercury exaggerated.
Mounts of Venus and Sun well-developed.

Fork

When there is a fork at the end of a line, it gives greater power to the line. This, however, is not true in the case of Line of Life.

Forked Fate

When the Line of Fate divides, and one branch touches the Mount of Venus while the other goes to the Mount of Moon, a journey or voyage is likely to take place under the influence of a member of the opposite sex.

—*Henry Frith*

Formation, Chained

A chained formation in any line is a sign of weakness. On the Life Line it shows bad health, on the Head Line instability of ideas, on the Heart Line changeability.

Fourth Finger, Qualities of

Too long—craftiness.
Too short—thoughtlessness.
Fair size—versatility.
Crooked—dishonesty.

Leaning towards the third—business with art.
Equal to first—talent for diplomacy.
Equal to second—scientific skill.
Equal to third—political influence.

Friendship of the Powerful People

Crosses on the second phalanx of the first finger.
Line from the Quadrangle to the Mount of Mercury
Line of Fate terminating on the Mount of Jupiter or Sun.
Mounts of Jupiter and Sun predominant.

Frivolity

Lower Mount of Mars absent or insignificant.
Line of Sun fragmentary.
A poor Line of Head.
First phalanx of the thumb weak.
Second finger short and pointed.

Frustration

The Line of Life terminating in a series of crosses at both the ends.
A poor Line of Fate.

Future of Palmistry

Not that the last word has yet been written upon this weighty subject, so infinitely varied in its capacity; that the last word shall never be penned so long as baby boys and baby girls will open their wondering eyes to the light of this world of ours. *New hands, new discoveries*: the whole of Palmistry is condensed in these four words.

—*Comte C. de Saint-Germain*

G

Gambler, Habitual

A very drooping Line of Head.
Large Mount of Moon.
Third finger equal to the second.
Short smooth fingers.
Soft hand.

Gastric Fever

Gastric fever is indicated by a red dot on the Hepatica or the Line of Liver.

Generative Functions, Troubles in

Troubles in the generative functions are indicated by the first bracelet high-up and convex in shape.

Generosity, The Quadrangle of

The Quadrangle formed in the centre of the palm is an indication of generous spirit and a strong inflexible will. This was shown in the hand of King Albert I of Belgium.

Genius

A much-developed Mount of the Sun.

George Bernard Shaw, Hand of

George Bernard Shaw had the line of intellect and wit. The Line of Intellect and Wit rises from the centre of the palm upward to the base of the third finger. It denotes an original and sparkling personality. This line is very rarely seen on the hand.

Giddiness

The Line of Head rising towards the Line of Heart.

Girdle of Venus, Readings from

The Girdle of Venus starts from between the first and second finger and ends between the third and fourth finger
Deep and red—defective intellect.
Terminating on the Mount of Mercury—great energy.
Star—venereal disease.
Double or triple—unnatural vices.
Thin and cut—lots of trouble.

Glorious Career

The Line of Sun ending in three equal branches, one towards the Mount of Sun, the other towards the Mercury and the third towards the Saturn.

Golden Rules of Palmistry

1. Apply yourself seriously to the Science of Palmistry.
2. Give your judgment after minute examination of the hand.
3. Use a great care in expressing your opinion.
4. Do not read hands in a crowd.
5. Do not read hands for the sake of amusement.
6. Do not try to humiliate the subject.
7. Never alarm a nervous person.
8. Point out remedies along with the maladies.
9. Never predict date of death
10. Always think of benefitting the subject.

Gonorrhoea

Gonorrhoea is indicated by the abnormal prominence of the Mount of Venus or when it is criss-crossed by confused lines.

Good Fortune

The Lines of Head and Heart forked under the Mount of Jupiter.

Gout

It is also known as "Satin skin".
  The Line of Life forked at the termination.
  The Line of Life red.
  Cross on the Mount of Moon.
  Mount of Moon exaggerated.
  Mount of Moon much lined.
  Exaggerated Mount of Jupiter.
  Mount of Jupiter much lined.

Great Love

Great love is indicated when the Line of Liver and the Milky Way (Via Lasciva) run as sister lines.

Great Palmer Arch

This Mount (of Venus), the Science of Physiology teaches, covers one of the most important blood vessels in the palm, viz., the Great Palmer Arch. If this loop or arch is large, it indicates a plentiful supply of blood and strong active circulation; consequently the health is more robust. It is found that persons possessing this mount well-developed, being in active strong health, are naturally more full of love than individuals in poor health, and who, in consequence, have this portion of the hand, either flat or poorly developed. Hence, when this mount is large, it has been considered to show passion and larger sensuality than when flat, flabby or non-developed.

—*Cheiro*

Greed

The Line of Heart crossing the palm.
The Mounts of Mercury and Sun exaggerated.
The third phalanx of every finger long and thick.

—Greta Garbo, Hand of

The Line of Emotional Moods encircles the base of the first finger, and it is significant of the power of expressing emotions in either dramatic or musical productions.

—Josef Ranald

Grille

A grille is a number of lines crossing one another at right angles. It is a serious menace. If the lines are deep and red, it shows an impending danger.

Grille, Qualities of

On the Mount of Luna—life of anxiety.
On the Mount of Venus—danger of imprisonment.
On the Mount of Jupiter—matrimonial unhappiness
On the Mount of Saturn—misfortunes.
On the Mount of Apollo—visionary idealism.
On the Mount of Mercury—dishonesty.
On the Mount of Mars—violent death.

Grille on Venus

This generally indicates an increase of Venusian qualities, particularly the sexual appetites.

—William G. Benham

Guilty Conscience

A black dot on the Line of Head.
A line of influence ending in a star on the Line of Head.

H

Hair and Health

The most superficial character-reader must have observed how certain temperaments accord with the complexion and general appearance of the individual. Fair-haired people are usually of a bright, sunny, sanguine nature. Those with red hair and florid complexion are hasty, passionate and strong. Dark-haired people are serious, sometimes melancholy. People with brown hair and eyes have great warmth of affection. Grey-eyed people are clever, as a rule, but their disposition is cold.

—*E. Rene*

Hair, Meaning of

Hairy female hand denotes cruelty.
Hairy male hand shows violent nature.
Hair on thumb shows inherited genius for inventiveness.
Hair on two lower phalanges of fingers—affection.
Hair on all phalanges—ardent disposition.
Dark-coloured hair—passionate nature

Hamlet

Dangerous morbidness and a tendency to suicide, of-to-be-or-not-to-be Hamlet type, is indicated by an exaggerated Mount of Saturn.

Hand

The hand is the organ of organs, the active agent of the passive powers of the entire system.

—*Aristotle*

The hand is the servant of the brain. By continual use, the nerves from the brain to the hand have become highly developed. Our hands are the photographic plates upon which our brain writes our impulses, whether good or bad.

—*Frances Kienzle*

He sealeth up the hand of every man, that all men may know his work.   —*Job*. Chapter 37, Verse 7

Length of days are in her right hand, riches and honour in her left.   —*Proverbs*: Chapter 3, Verse 16.

The superiority of man is owing to his hands.

—*Anaxgoras*

There is ample proof to be found that the hand mirrors not only the character of an individual but his aims and ambitions—and even more importantly, his possibilities of achieving them.

—*Rita Van Alen*

The only thing that the human hand cannot do is to create an instrument as perfect as itself.

—*W. G. Benham*

In the hand every single bone is distinguishable from one another; each digit has its own peculiar character.

—*Sir Richard Owen*

Well, if God has printed to the eye of certain clear-seeing minds, the destiny of each man, on his physiognomy—taking this word as meaning the total expression of the body—why should not the hand give the characteristics of the physiognomy, since the hand contains the whole of the human acting and its only medium of manifestation?

—*Balzac*
Le Gousin Pons

Hand, Hair on

Soft hair on the hand denote an effeminate nature. The person is sensitive, imaginative, affectionate. Rough wiry hair denote a rough wiry character.

Hand-Reading

1. In males see the right hand; in females the left hand.
2. In males the left hand shows inherited qualities. The reverse is the case with the females.
3. If the subject is left-handed, reverse the process stated above.
4. If the subject is ambidextrous, read both hands.

Hands, Different Kinds of

There are hands which naturally attract us, and there are hands which excite in us repulsion. I have seen hands which seemed covered with eyes, so sagacious and penetrating was their appearance. Some, like those of the sphinx, suggest an idea of mystery; some betray recklessness and strength, combined with activity of the body; others, again, indicate laziness, joined to feebleness and cunning.

—*D'Arpentigny*

Handshake, Qualities of

Soft and flabby—love of luxury.
Firm and of even pressure—dependability, discipline, ambition.
Hard and hurting—affectionate with strong likes and dislikes.

Happiness, Domestic

A cross on the Mount of Jupiter.
A straight, clear, uncrossed Line of Fate rising from the Rascette.

Happy Career

One straight line on the third phalanx of the third finger.

Happy-Go-Lucky Fellow

Hand thick and soft.
Mounts of Jupiter and Venus well-developed.
No worry lines.

Harmony of Existence

If all the mounts are evenly or equally developed, it indicates a desirable harmony of existence. It is the hand of peace and plenty.

Hay Fever

Poor Line of Liver.
Narrow Quadrangle.
Line of Heart curving to the Line of Head.

Headaches

Small breaks on the Line of Head.
Bars cutting the Line of Head.
Line of Head short.
Line of Liver irregular.
Line of Head chained.
Line of Liver red at the end.
Line of Head drooping.
Line of Head cut by many bars.

Headaches, Serious

Drooping and much broken Line of Head.
"Very large branch from starting point of the Line of Life down to the Rascette."

—Germain

Head, Double Line of

Cheiro had a double Line of Head. This is what he says about it:

"A double Line of Head is very rarely found. The character shown by each of these lines of Head is in an apparent contradiction to the other. For example, the lower closely joined to the Line of Life denotes a mentality extremely sensitive, artistic and imaginative. The upper line gives the reverse characteristics."

Head Line, Readings from

Straight and stiff—commercial cleverness.
Running close to the Line of Life—brain trouble.
Running close to the Line of Heart—asthma.
Absence of Head Line—idiocy.
Short and faint—lack of concentration.
Thin—brain trouble.
Narrow and weak—frivolity.
Wavy and uneven—fickle mentality.
Chained—chronic headaches.
Pale and broad—dull intellect.
Long and straight—love of details.
Forked termination—imagination controlled by reason.
Bars—headaches.
Break—wound in the head.
Very broken—loss of memory.
Knotted—tendency to murder.
White spots—discoveries.
Dark spots—typhoidal character.
Cross—grave accident.
Triangle—success in science.
Island—lung trouble.
Accompanied by a sister line—inheritance.

Headstrong

When the Head and the Heart lines merge and make one long line across the hand, the person is headstrong and his head rules over his heart.

Head, The Perfect

Rising from the Mount of Jupiter and yet touching the Line of Life, it is, if a long Line of Head, the most powerful of all. Such a person will have talent, energy, and daring determination of purpose, with boundless ambition combined with reason. Such a person will control others, yet not seem to control them; he will have caution even in the most daring designs; he takes pride in the management of people or things, and is strong in rule, but just in the administration of power.

—*Cheiro*

Head Wounds on

Very small lines on the Mount of Jupiter.
A star on the Line of Head.

Health Hints

Particularly as regards health and the disease to affect the subject, the nails will be found to be remarkably sure guides. Medical men both in London and Paris have taken up this study of the nails with great interest. Often a patient does not know, or for the moment forgets, what his parents have suffered or died from; but an examination of the nails will in a few seconds disclose important hereditary traits.

—*Cheiro*

Heartlessness

The Line of Heart branchless and straight.
Mounts of Sun and Venus very small.

Line of Head cutting the hand like a bar.
Long finger of Saturn.
Hand thin and hard.

Heart Line, Readings from

Absence of line—extreme coldness of heart.
Long line—idealistic love.
Very red—violence in love.
Livid—liver trouble.
Very deep—threat of apoplexy.
Very pale and white—heart disease.
Thin and long—murderous instinct.
Chained—love trouble.
Weak and poorly traced—faithlessness.
Chained—flirtation.
Frayed—love worries.
Downward branches—love disappointments.
Much broken—contempt for the opposite sex.
Bars—disappointments.
Dots—love sorrows.
Red scar—apoplexy.
Circle—weakness of heart.
Island—intrigue.

Heart Palpitations

Line of Liver red at the start.
Line of Liver connected with the Line of Life.
Dots on the Line of Heart.

Heart Troubles

Bars cutting the Line of Heart.
Line of Heart broken.
Chained Line of Heart.
Lines of Influence from the Mount of Venus cutting the Line of Heart.
Mount of Sun exaggerated.
Mount of Sun much lined.

Nails short, square and bluish.
Plain of Mars hollow towards the Heart Line.
Lines of Life and Liver closely connected.
Red or bluish spots on the Line of Life.
The Line of Heart broken under the Mount of Mercury.

Heart Weakness

A circle on the Line of Heart.
Line of Heart pale and wide.
Line of Liver wavy.
Line of Head poor.
Total absence of the Line of Heart.
Pale skin.
Narrow thin palm.
Short and square nails.

Hæmorrhage

A star on the Mount of Moon.
Line of Heart poor or absent.
Grille on the Upper Mount of Mars.

Hemorrhoids

Exaggerated Mount of Saturn.
Mount of Saturn much lined.
Line of influence from dot on the Line of Life.
A branch from the Line of Life ending in a star on the Upper Mount of Mars.

Hepatica

The Hepatica has been differently described as the Line of Liver, the Line of Mercury, the Line of Health or the Line of Disease. Normally it rises from the Mount of Moon and runs along the percussion. It is on the whole a tragic line and it is best not to have it. The Hepatica rising from the Line of Life is the worst indication possible.

Hepatica, Qualities of

The qualities of Hepatica are good or bad, according to its character. If the line is deep, it reveals excellent disposition, vitality, healthy constitution, good memory, clear brain and healthy operation of the intellectual faculties. The results are the opposite if the order is reversed.

A broad and shallow Hepatica denotes lack of vitality which results in stomach and liver trouble. The subject becomes despondent and a victim of occasional outbursts of headaches and dyspepsia.

If the line is chained, the subject tends to suffer from gall, duct, gall stones, cirrhosis and other liver troubles which may even prove fatal.

Hiding Habits

It may be stated here that the hand whose owner has little or nothing to hide opens itself freely to the gaze, and that the hand of one whose deeds and thoughts will not bear the inspection wishes to hide itself, or to close the fingers over the palm, studiously concealing it from sight. The mind feels the necessity of hiding its workings and the fingers, obeying the suggestion, close over the palm.

—*William G. Benham*

Hindu Interpretation

The Hindus have an elaborate system of using these lines of influence, and depend on them for a large part of their work. Only the lines which run inside the Life Line are properly the Lines of Influence, and I have found they indicate persons who have strongly influenced the life either for good or ill, and that they generally represent members of one's family or the closest friends.

—*William G. Benham*

Hindu Science

Palmistry is essentially an Indian science. The ancient Hindus were the first discoverers of Palmistry Cheiro has acknowledged this many times in his books:—

"To consider the origin of this science, we must take our thoughts back to the earliest days of the world's history, and furthermore to the consideration of a people the oldest of all, yet one that has survived the fall of empires, nations and dynasties, and who are today as characteristic and as full of individuality as they were thousands of years ago when the first records of history were written. I allude to those children of the East, the Hindus, a people whose philosophy and wisdom are being everyday revived.

LANGUAGE OF THE HAND

Hollow Palm

A hollow palm, if at the same time, hard, is an unfortunate sign. There is just a hidden something about such a person that generally attracts ill-luck and disappointment.

—Cheiro
YOU AND YOUR HAND

Honesty, Want of

A wavy Line of Head.
A narrow triangle.
An exaggerated Mount of Mercury.

Housewife, The Excellent

The Line of Head moderately long
Very few lines beside the Main Lines
Mounts of Venus and Mercury pronounced.
Long Line of Heart starting deep into the Mount of Jupiter.

Mounts moderate.
Nails short.
Fingers square.
First knot of fingers quite marked.
Palm elastic.
Palm and fingers even.

Husband, Ideal

Long Heart Line, with branches rising on to Jupiter.
A straight finger of Jupiter.
A well-developed spatulate or square thumb.
Mounts of Venus and Luna well placed.
A clear deep Head Line.
Straight fingers.
A firm hand.

Hydrophobia

A star on the Mount of Moon in both hands.

Hypersensitiveness

When the right hand of a person is drooping and the left swaying, it indicates hypersensitiveness. It shows an excess of feminity. Such a person is finicky in the extreme.

Hypnotism

Great qualities of hypnotism are shown by the Upper Mars leading towards the Mount of Moon.

Hypochondriac

A person who imagines himself habitually ill is called the hypochondriac. It is indicated by the following signs:—

Mount of Moon exaggerated.
Line of Head drooping into the Mount of Moon.
The Medical Stigmata clearly marked.

Hysteria

Girdle of Venus cut by many bars.
Double or triple Girdle of Venus.
Second finger crooked.
Star on the Mount of Moon.
Line of influence connecting Mount of Moon with the Mount of Venus.

I

Idealism

Enthusiasm for the highest ideals is shown by:
Mounts of Sun and Moon predominant.
Drooping Line of Head.
High Mount of Moon.
The Mount of Jupiter fine.
The first finger excellent.
Thin soft hands with pointed fingers.

Idealistic Temperament

Mount of Jupiter very prominent.
First phalanx of the first finger above normal.
Almond-shaped nails.
Slender palm.
Palm shorter than fingers.
Pointed finger tips.

Ideal Love

Ideal Love is characterized by a long and narrow Line of Head starting high up from the Mount of Jupiter.

Idiocy

Often one of the main lines missing.
Very poor Line of Heart.
Line of Head drooping, broken and twisted.
The Mounts of Moon and Mars bulging.
A very ill-shaped hand.
Dwarfed thumb.
Ill-formed fingers.

Illegitimate Birth

Poor Line of Fate.

Island at the start of Fate Line.
Island at the start of Life Line.

Ill Health

Dots on the Line of Life.
Line of Liver connected with the Line of Life.
Line of Life formed of ladderlike fragments.
Thin palm.
Wide and pale Line of Life.
Line of Life chained or linked.
Line of Fate twisted.
Line of Fate crossed at the start.
Star on the Mount of Saturn.
Lines of Life and Fate intertwined at the start.
Cross at the end of the Line of Life.
Short and broad Line of Liver.
A portion of Life Line thin.

Illness

Break, cross, star or black dot on the Line of Life.
Break, cross, star or black dot on the Line of Liver.
A semicircular line cutting Line of Life
A bar cutting Line of Life

Illness from Love

Branches connecting Lines of Life and Heart indicate illness caused by love sickness.

Illness from Sorrows

Illness due to an overwhelming sorrow is indicated by a line from the Mount of Mars crossing the Line of Heart.

Illusion

According to De Peruccio, "a star-shaped white mark" on nails indicate self-deception, an illusion of life, and unrequitted love.

Imagination, Creative

A perfect broad Triangle.
Well-developed Mounts of Moon and Venus.
Mounts of Jupiter and Sun excellent.
Almond-shaped nails.
First phalanx of fingers very long.
Soft hand.
Palm smaller than fingers.
Pointed finger tips.

Imagination, Unhealthy

Hands thin and very soft, almost transparent.
Mount of Venus exaggerated.
Line of Head drooping and widely forked.
Strong Girdle of Venus.

Imagination with Practicality

Hands and fingers of equal length.
Conical finger tips.
Line of Head drooping very little.
Mounts of Moon and Venus moderate.
Mounts of Sun and Moon blended.
Second knot of fingers marked.
Palm elastic.

Immorality

An exaggerated Mount of Venus.
A star on the first phalanx of the thumb.

Imprudence

Mount of Saturn very small.
Second finger conical.
Smooth short fingers.
Short first phalanx of the thumb.
Lines of Life and Head widely separated at the start.

Impulsiveness

People with thumbs bending back are impulsive children of nature. Their sense of morals does not play much part in their lives. Other Signs:

        Fingers thrown backwards.
        Fingers naturally flexible.

Also see "Imprudence"

Inability to Keep Secrets

When the hands of a person are limp and dangling, it indicates indecision, aimlessness and inability to keep valuable secrets.

Inconstancy

    A crescent inside the Triangle.
    Cross lines on the Lower Mount of Mars.
    A short Line of Head.
    A chained Line of Heart.
    First phalanx of the thumb below normal.
    Soft hands.
    Fingers smooth and conically tipped.

Independence of Character

    Plain of Mars well marked.
    Mounts of Mars prominent.
    Long Line of Head.
    Line of Head separated from the Line of Life at the start.
    Mount of Jupiter predominant.
    Long first phalanx of the thumb.
    Short nails.
    Knotted fingers.
    Fingers spatulate-tipped.
    Wide space between bases of first and second fingers.
    First finger leaning towards the thumb.

Independence of Spirit

When the thumb stands at right angle to the palm, the person possesses a great independence of spirit. He cannot brook opposition. Little jerks will make him fly to the extremes.

Indigestion, Habitual

Poor Line of Head.
Wavy Line of Liver.
Line of Life islanded.

Indomitable Determination

The Line of Indomitable Determination starts at the side of the hand below the first finger.

Infantile Diseases

With every Life Line we find the first years chained or poorly marked in some way. This shows the period of life covered by infantile diseases.

—*William G Benham*

Influence, Ascending

Small branches which go upwards from the main lines are lines of ascending influence.

Influence, Descending

Small lines which go downwards from the main lines are lines of descending influence.

Influence Line, Influence of

When an influence line begins deep and then grows thin, until it gradually fades away, the influence was strong in the beginning, but has gradually grown weaker until it has no effect.

—*William G. Benham*

Influence Lines

Lines of Influence are tiny lines that go upwards or downwards from the main lines or mounts, cut or cross the lines or merely touch them or terminate in various signs on the palm.

Influence Lines of Life

These influence lines run parallel to the Life Line, on the thumb side. These lines represent people who have had a strong influence on career and character, such as the parents.

Inheritance

An acute angle cutting the first bracelet of the Rascette.

Inheritance, Rich

A long sister line to the Line of Head.
Star on the first bracelet of the Rascette.
Cross within the Triangle.

Insanity

A split Line of Head.
Line of Head merging into the Line of Liver.
Line of Life forked at the start.
Line of Head sloping deeply.
Line of Head deeply broken.
Wavy Line of Head.
Line of Head rising close to the Line of Heart
Line of Head sloping to the Mount of Moon.
The sign of moon on the Mount of Moon.
The sign of moon on the Mount of Saturn.
Mount of Moon bulging.
Confused lines on the Mount of Moon.
Line of Head starred or chained.
Star on second phalanx of second finger.

Insult, Life of

A star on the Mount of Mercury.

Intellectual Ability

Excellent Lines of Head and Liver.
Long Line of Heart.
Line of Heart sloping.
Line of Heart forked.
Superb Line of Head.
Mounts of Sun, Jupiter and Mercury predominant.
Fingers longer than palm.
Fingers conical.
Fingers knotted.

Intellect, Measure of

Measure the thumb with the first finger. The higher it goes over the base of the finger, the higher the intellectual capacity of the subject. This extraordinary fact has been completely demonstrated by Sir Charles Bell in his work relating to the paw of a chimpanzee.

—Cheiro

COMFORT'S PALMISTRY GUIDE

Interlinked Head and Heart Lines

It is not a good sign when the Head Line leaves its natural course and rises up to join the Heart Line. Cheiro says thus:

"Many palmists say that it indicates criminality. It does not always indicate criminality, as I have seen a few who had these lines merging and were not criminals. In every case, however, I will say that they are headstrong, desiring to have their own way and regarding little the feelings or rights of others. They very often have good qualities to keep them from giving away entirely to their baser qualities."

Internal Trouble

Fullness of the Mount of Moon.
Islands on the Line of Liver.

Intestinal Trouble

Large island at the termination of the Line of Head
Strong red line between first and second fingers.
Mount of Mars much lined.
Mount of Moon rayed.

Intolerance

Heart and Head lines running close together show impatience and intolerance.

Intrepidity

A fine Line of Heart.
Fine Mount of Mercury.
Plain of Mars wide.
Mount of Mars predominant.
Thumb rather short.
First phalanx of thumb rather long.
Third finger above normal.
Square palm.
Smooth spatulate fingers.
Strong square nails.

Intrigues, Guilty

An island on the line of influence from the Mount of Venus.
A branch from the Line of Life cutting the Line of Heart.
An island on the Line of Fate.
An island on the Line of Heart.
An island on the Line of Marriage.
An island on the Mount of Venus.

Intuition, Gift of

A triangle on the Mount of Moon.
Drooping Line of Head.
Line of Fate rising from the Mount of Moon.
A fine Triangle.
A clear Line of Intuition.
A clear Line of Liver.
Thin and very soft hands.
Short nails
Short smooth conical fingers.
First phalanges of fingers long.
First phalanx of thumb short.
Mounts of Moon and Mercury predominant.
Mount of Saturn strongly marked.
Thumb conical.

Intuition, The Line of

This line is included within the boundaries of the Mount of Moon. It is also called the Line of Moon. It gives an individual an insight into the unknown and warns him against the coming dangers.

Intuitive Power

A whorl under the first finger denotes a great gift of intuitive power.

Inventive Genius, Practical

A fine Line of Head slightly drooping.
Line of Head with triple fork at the end.
Mounts of Mercury and Sun predominant.
A long thumb.
Fourth finger above normal.
Long knotted fingers.
Short nails.
Elastic palm

Inventive Genius, Unpractical

Confused downward lines on the Mounts of Sun and Mercury.
Line of Head drooping on the Mount of Moon.
Fingers without knots.

Irony, Gift of

Short nails.
Soft palm.
Mount of Mercury predominant.
A poor Line of Heart.

Irresponsibility

First finger too short.
First phalanx of thumb below normal.
Mounts of Mars insignificant.
Line of Head attached a pretty distance with the Line of Life.

Irritability

One who bites his nails is irritable and has an excitable temperament. He is rather childish in his behaviour. These are his signs:
A deeply red coloured line of Mars.
Red Skin.
Exaggerated Mounts and Plain of Mars.
Hair on all phalanges.
Dark coloured hair on hand.
Thick hard palm.
Short, broad and red nails.

Island

An island is a sign of defect. The extent of the defect depends upon the extent of the island.

Islanded Affection Line

An islanded Affection Line (Line of Marriage) denotes interruption or unhappiness during the course of affection. If there are more than one island, the response is not strong enough to cause a matrimonial alliance.

Islanded Fate Line

An islanded Fate Line indicates that the career of the subject was interrupted because of his nefarious leanings towards infidelity and depravity.

Islanded Influence Line

An islanded Influence Line, which runs parallel to the main line, tells of a subject whose influence is not very wholesome in its effects, and if the line ends in a star, dot, cross or cross bar, the influence ceases altogether.

Islanded Mercury Line

An island on the Mercury Line is a grave defect. It indicates appendicitis or other serious stomach trouble. It also shows that Head, Heart and other vital organs are defective.

Islands, Qualities of

On the Life Line—severe illness.
On any influence line—sorrow.
On the Hepatica—internal illness.
On the Line of Apollo—loss of money.
On the Head Line—delirium.
On the Heart Line—disease.
On the Fate Line—unhappy attachment.

J

Jack of all Trades

When thumbs are set very low in the hand, the subject indicated is a Jack of all trades—and master of none!

Jaundice

> Mount of Mercury exaggerated.
> Mount of Mercury much lined.
> A spot or star on the Mount of Moon.

Jealousy

> A long Line of Heart.
> A high Mount of Moon.
> A Girdle of Venus.

Judge's Hand

> Good Head Line.
> Long conic fingers.
> A wide Quadrangle.
> Long first phalanx of Mercury.
> Good Mount of Apollo.
> Straight Jupiter finger.

Jupiterian Type

A person with the Mount of Jupiter predominant is called the Jupiterian. He is ambitious but a very pleasant person. He is expansive, gay and self-confident. He is strong and well-built. He is basically honest. He has an idealistic attitude towards life. The Jupiterians are born to command. They are excellent leaders in business, politics and army.

Jupiter, Qualities of the Mount

Normal—Spiritual ideals, honest pride, love of great adventure.

Above Normal—Superstition, artistic conceit, vanity, boasting.

Below Normal—Disgust for religion, contempt of others, absence of self-respect.

K

Key to Character

Any one Mount that is more highly developed than the others gives a key to the nature of the individual. This main mount must often be considered with an auxiliary mount. By this is meant, where there are two or more mounts of about the same size or development, the meaning of each mount must be analysed, synthesized, and deductions drawn. It must be understood that only in this manner may a hand be placed in its proper category and intelligent deductions arrived at.

—*Alice Denton Jennings*

Kidney Trouble

A long line of Voyage forked at the end.
Line of Voyage touching the Line of Life.
Mount of Moon exaggerated.
Mount of Moon much lined.
Cross on the Mount of Moon.

Knotted Fingers

The following deductions are made from the knotted fingers:—
    Knotted pointed fingers — inventive inspiration.
    Knotted conical fingers — topical genius.
    Knotted square fingers — financial wizardry.
    Knotted spatulate fingers — sportsmanship.

Knotty-Fingered People

These knotty-fingered people are well-named philosophical, as they are hunting for truth. They do not analyse from any frivolous motive, but because they wish to arrive at the facts, so while they do not seem to respond as quickly as smooth-fingered subjects, always remember that they are honestly striking to get at the bottom of the matter, and will be guided by the result of their investigations as the facts may appear to them.

—*William G. Benham*

L

Lady Luck

The Line of Apollo indicates wealth, fortune, and the "Lady Luck" that brings health and happiness.

Late Success

Success late in life is indicated by a cross inside the lower part of the triangle.

Law, Success in

A line from the Rascette to the Mount of Jupiter.

Lawyer, Qualities of

Line of Head separated from the Line of Life at the start.
Line of Head forked at the termination.
Large Mounts of Mercury and Mars.
Long second phalanx of the thumb.
Fourth finger predominant.
Short nails.
Long straight thumb.
Fingers long and close.
Straight Head Line.
Flat palm.

Laziness

Drooping Line of Head.
Short first phalanx of the Thumb.
Mounts of Moon, Venus, and Sun predominant.
Very short conical fingers.
Hand thick and soft.
Palm larger than fingers.

Legacies

Star on the first bracelet of the Rascette.
Line of Influence from a star on the Mount of Venus.
Lines of Influence from the Mount of Moon.

(*Further see* "Inheritance")

Legs, Wounds on

Very small lines on the Mount of Saturn.
Cross lines on the Mount of Mercury.
Dark spots on the Mount of Mercury.
Mount of Saturn exaggerated.
Mount of Saturn much lined.
Line of Head broken under the Mount of Saturn

Length of Hand

Palm longer than fingers—self-indulgence, laziness, idle dreaming
Palm and fingers equal in length—harmonious development.
Palm shorter than fingers—idealism and imagination.

Length of Life

Almost every one thinks that the length of Life Line is a sure proof of the length of life. This presupposition is a mistake. There are many other things to be taken into account.

Lethargy

A very low plain of Mars.
Single uncrossed bracelet of the Rascette.
Very poor Line of Life.
Line of Heart weak.

Liar

The Line of Head drooping.
The Line of Head forked

No Mount of Jupiter.
Fourth finger crooked.
Mount of Moon exaggerated
Mount of Mercury rayed.
Cross on the Mount of Mercury.

Liberality

Mount of Jupiter most prominent.
Mount of Venus exaggerated.
Well-proportioned palm.
Well-proportioned fingers.
Square finger-tips.
Excellent thumb.
Finely-shaped Quadrangle.
Line of Head long.
Life Line slightly separated from the Head Line at the start.
Life Line slightly forked.

Licentiousness

The Via Lasciva, a sister line of the Line of Liver, indicates unbridled sensuality and boundless passion. When it cuts through the Line of Life, it indicates death through licentiousness. The Via Lasciva is indicative of extreme vitality which necessarily finds an outlet in lascivious practices.

Life Line, Law of

As a general proposition, the longer the Line of Life, the longer will be the life of the subject, and the shorter the line, the shorter it will be.

—*William G. Benham*

Life Love-Lorn

Lines rising from the Mount of Venus and cutting the lines of Life, Head and Heart

Life, Map of

Life Line is the map of the natural course of the subject's life. The absence of a Life Line simply shows that the life of the subject hangs only by a hair, and for such a one Death is a visitor who may come at any moment.

—*Benham*

Life, Measurement of

Measure the Life Line with a thread from the Rascette to the starting point below the first finger. If the Life Line does not reach up to the Rascette, still you measure up to that point. Then double the thread and mark the middle point with ink. Then divide each half into five equal parts. The marks indicate the following ages:—

First Mark	6th year.
Second Mark	12th year.
Third Mark	18th year.
Fourth Mark	24th year.
Fifth Mark	30th year.
Sixth Mark	36th year.
Seventh Mark	43rd year.
Eighth Mark	51st year.
Ninth Mark	60th year.
Tenth Mark	70th year.

Life, Readings from the Line of

Forming a great circle on the palm—long life.
Short in both hands—early death.
Chained—nervous trouble.
Livid colour—morbidity.
Very deep—fast living.
Deep and red—violent disposition.
Thin—ill-health.
Forked at the start—justice.

Abrupt termination—sudden death.
Separated from Head Line—extreme action.
Starting from the Mount of Jupiter—great ambition.
Upward branches—healthful influences.
Downward branches—unhealthful influences.
Break—serious illness.
Laddered—continuous illness.
Cut—illness.
Dot—casualty.
Bluish spot—typhoid.
Island on the line—serious trouble.
Red dots—feverish disposition.
Black dots—grave disease.
Cross—accident.

Life Ruined by Love

Double Line of Heart.
Lines of Fate and Sun poor.
Lines of Fate and Sun starred.
A wavy Line of Head.
Line of Head running towards the Line of Heart.
Line of Fate merging into a broken or starred Line of Heart under the Mount of Saturn.

Life Ruined Through Imprudence

Exaggerated Mount of Moon.
Line of Head drooping to the Mount of Moon.
Line of Fate from the Mount of Moon.
Line of Fate stopping at the Line of Heart.
Third finger longer than the second.
Second finger below normal.
Widely separated Lines of Life and Head.

Limpidity of Truth

As says Comte de Saint-Germain, while studying Palmistry, we must try to arrive at the "very limpidity of truth". We must not permit ourselves to be hampered by any antiquarian authoritarianism. It is delicate to ventilate upon the "how" and "why" of the lines accepted as such since times immemorial, but that does not deprive us of the right to offer the most sensible interpretation. Lines should not be taken as the gospel truth. Even a beginner has a right to improve upon the interpretations on the basis of his own intuition, commonsense, experience and study.

Line of Longevity

The Line of Longevity, called the Life Line, begins under the first finger. It runs down the palm and encircles the base of the thumb. The extraordinary length of this line indicates longevity.

Lines

Eminent psychologists and physiologists the world over agree that, along with convulsions of the brain, the lines in the palm of the hand serve as an index to the personality of every man, woman and child.

—Josef Ranald

Perhaps there exists between the phenomenon of the nervous system and of electricity a sympathy of connection at present unknown, analogous to that which has been found to exist between electricity and magnetism.

—Muller

Lines have not been traced without cause in the hands of men; they evidently emanate from the influence of heaven and from human individuality.

—Aristotle

Ideas are nothing but vibrations, nothing but changes occurring within us, and they are caused by some external influence transmitted through the nerves to the cerebral fibres.

—*Charles Bonnet*

Around the man's nerves there does exist an invisible atmosphere.

—*Alexander von Humbolt*

Lines, Main and Minor

There are seven main lines and seven minor lines in a hand. The main lines are: the Life Line, the Head Line, the Heart Line, the Fate Line, the Apollo Line, the Mercury Line and the Saturn Line. The minor lines are: the Girdle of Venus, the Line of Marriage, the Ring of Solomon, the Ring of Saturn, the Bracelets, the Line of Intuition and the Line of Mars.

Lines, Minute

Give as much importance to minute lines as to the main ones. There is a tendency to skip over small lines and hit highlights. The results will be sad and bad. By overlooking minute signs you will miss a wealth of information for the formulation of correct judgment.

Literary Success

The Line of Sun good.
A cross on the finger of Jupiter.
A star or white spot on the Mount of Sun.
Girdle of Venus good.
Branch of the Fate Line going to the Mount of Mercury.

Literature, Aptitude for

A line from Rascette straight up to the Mount of Moon.

Small downward line on the first joint of the first finger.
Drooping Line of Head.
Line of Head forked at the termination.
White dots on the Line of Head.
Long first and fourth fingers.
Fingers conical.
Mounts of Mercury and Sun predominant.
Mounts of Moon and Venus predominant for poetry and fiction.

Liver Line, Readings from

The Line of Liver, also called the Line of Mercury, starts from above the Rascette without touching the Line of Life and goes straight up to the Mount of Mercury.

Long and deep—longevity and success.
Starting from percussion—changeable behaviour.
Absent—alert disposition.
Laddered—liver trouble.
Breaks—illnesses.
Wavy—biliousness.
Yellow—liver trouble.
Red—bad headache.
Straight and thin—stiffness of manners.
Thick and short—bad digestion.
Large island—somnabulism.
Deep bars—illnesses.

Liver Trouble

Dark spots on the Mount of Moon.
Line of Liver laddered.
Lines yellow-coloured.
Mount of Mercury exaggerated.
Mount of Mercury much lined.
Damp skin.

Longevity

Life Line—clear and deep.
Heart Line—clear and deep.
Bracelets—clear and unbroken.
Liver Line—not cutting the Life Line.
Great Triangle (formed by Head, Heart and Liver Lines)—free from criss-cross lines.
Rascette—complete
Liver Line—long and clear.
Fate Line—long and good.

Loss of Blood

A wavy Line of Head starting downward from the first and second finger.

Love, Boundless

A large Mount of Venus.
Hands generally soft.
A fine clear Line of Heart.
Via Lasciva as sister line to the Line of Liver.
A fine Line of Mars.
Line of Mars clear and red.
Mount of Mars strong.
Main lines red.
Line of Heart starting forkless under the Mount of Saturn.
Exaggerated Mounts of Venus and Moon.
Thick soft hand.

Love, Desire for

Strong Mount of Venus.
Smooth fingers.
The pointed tips.

Love Disappointed

Star in the Triangle.

Line of Fate chained when crossing the Line of Heart.
Line of Head running close to the Line of Heart.
Line of Heart cut by a bar near the start.
Plain of Mars hollow towards the Line of Heart.

Love for a Married Person

An island on the Line of Fate in both the hands.

Love for a near Relative

The Line of Marriage formed into islands.

Love for one Person only

Large cross on the Mount of Venus.
Clear cross on the Mount of Jupiter.

Love, Happiness in

A clear-cut Line of Heart, starting with a fork, one branch going up to the Mount of Jupiter.

A clear straight uncrossed line from the Mount of Venus to the Mount of Mercury.

Loveless Life

The Line of Life and the Line of Heart very far apart at the start and very branchless.

Love, Lordliest

When the Line of Heart rises from the Mount of Jupiter, or the first finger itself, it gives the capacity for the highest type of love, pure and paramount.

"Alas!" says Cheiro, "Such people are sufferers in the world of affection; when their idol falls, as idols will sometimes, the shock to their pride is so great that they rarely, if ever, recover from its ill-effects."

Love without Marriage

Short lines ascending from the Line of Fate to the Line of Heart.

Lower Mars, Qualities of the Mount

Normal—religious resignation, stoicism, patience, not afraid of anything.

Above Normal—Unhealthy self-torture, hard-heartedness, passive cruelty.

Below Normal—Sensitive soul, easily offended, afraid of pain, cowardice.

Lunarian Type

The person with the Mount of Moon predominant is called the Lunarian. He is an imaginative, dreamy child. He loves nature and daydreaming. The singing of the birds and the rustling of the leaves enchant him. Most of the writers, poets, and producers belong to this class. He loves travel and tries to run away from his habitual surroundings. He is fickle and moody. Food is a hobby with him. He eats while he thinks and thinks while he eats. He has a very strong imagination.

Lung Disease

Line of influence ending in an island on the Mount of Jupiter.
Many islands on the Line of Head.
Mount of Jupiter exaggerated.
Pale lines.
Thin Palm.
Long, brittle, curved, fluted nails.

Lust without Love

If the Line of Affection (or Marriage) is shallow or chained in a woman's hand, she has got no particular attachment for anyone. She chooses men, weighing them on the basis of the pleasure she derives. She is cold, selfish and cruel. If the line is white in colour, these qualities are highlighted.

M

Madame Curie, The Hand of

Madame Curie, the most famous woman scientist of the world, had the Line of Intuition which helped her to discover radium.

The Line of Intuition starts below the fourth finger on the side of the hand and takes a course in a semi-circular form, down the palm, denoting a highly intuitive mind and enables its possessor to solve sometimes baffling mysteries, where the keenest minds have been vainly searching for a solution.

Madman, Natural

Wide, sloping Line of Head.
Line of Head formed of islands and little hair-lines.
The Line of Head, made of short wavy branches.
Lines from one Mount of Mars to the other.
Nails short and red

Madness, Dangerous

Mounts of Moon and Mars exaggerated.
All lines very red.
The Line of Life of a livid colour.
The sign of Mars on the Mount of Moon.
The sign of Moon on the Mount of Mars.

Madness, Melancholy and Religious

The Line of Head descends with a sharp curve.
The Line of Head reaches low down on the Mount of Luna
The Mount of Venus is not well-developed.
The Mount of Saturn dominates.

Magnetism of Mounts

Extremes meet, and in so doing, supply deficiencies of character, or support the weaker, as the case may be. Mercurial people attract those of the temperament of Luna. Saturn and Apollo being of opposite natures, are magnetically attracted to each other. Mars and Venus have a liking for each other. Jupiter, being of a social disposition, is friendly with each and all.

—*E. Rene*

Main Lines Mixed

When the Head, Heart and Life Lines are all joined beneath the first finger in both hands, there is danger of an early or violent death.

—*Henry Frith*

Male Sexual Trouble

Troubles of the generative organs in males are indicated by:
  A star at the conjunction of the Lines of Head and Liver.
  First Bracelet of the Rascette very convex.
  Exaggerated Mount of Venus.
  Mount of Venus badly marked.

Man of Destiny

The Line of Life rising from Rascette and ending on the second phalanx of the second finger.

Many Love Affairs

Two parallel lines from the Mount of Venus to the Lower Mount of the Mars.

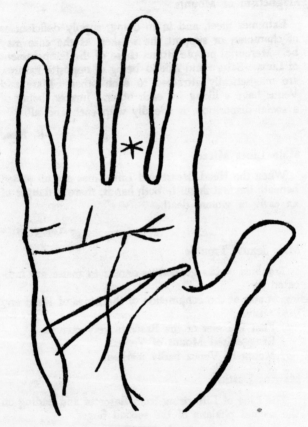

Gandhi's Hand

Mahatma Gandhi, The Hand of

"The Triangle of Wisdom is formed in the centre of the hand by the intersection of three lines, revealing an inner strength and wisdom which borders on the superman. And that wisdom and that moral strength which this triangle indicates has shown the world many times the great Mahatma or Great Soul of India. His is the wisdom of passive resistance and the strength to carry it out, as he struggles valiantly for the independence of his people, and obliteration of the caste system that made millions of untouchables, outcastes forced to a life of abject misery. Time and again the British authorities have thrown him into prison for his demonstrations, but still they have grudgingly been grateful to the Mahatma for his advocacy and enforcement of non-violent resistance. The power which he has attained has resulted from his extraordinary self-effacement. He holds that peace and love will solve all problems and he is resolved to do all in his power to make love a practical force in this world. His hand clearly shows the lines of imperial conquests, yet his indomitable will directs his destiny and he cares only for the power necessary to relieve his millions of followers from the inhuman caste system."

—*Josef Ranald*

Map of Life

Isn't it interesting to know that when we enter the world, we bring with us in our own two hands, our Life Map? A map that reveals our talents, characteristics, protentialities, likes and dislikes, in short, our destiny? We should never lose sight of the fact, however, that we have within ourselves the power over our mental attitude which we can develop towards happiness or despondency. Thank goodness, God gave us a will or mind which we can use to work with or against Fate.

—*Frances Kienzle*

Map of Mind

The zigzag lines on the palm of the hand may aptly be called the mighty map of mind. All our ideas and ideals, grand and grandiose, are outlined there in unmistakable hues and shades.

Marriage, Brilliant

A cross and star united on the Mount of Jupiter. Fine Line of Fate ending on the Mount of Jupiter. Line of Fate merging into good Line of Heart.

Marriage Frustration

The Line of Sun cut by the Line of Marriage.

Marriage, Happy

An island on the Line of Marriage with a cross-bar on the Line of Fate.

A line starting from a star on the Mount of Venus to the Line of Heart where it ends in a fork.

Marriage Influence

A line of influence that emerges from the Life Line sometime between the ages of 20 and 30 years is supposedly that of the husband or wife. If the marriage is happy, the line is deep and well-cut, denoting a dominating influence of the new-comer. If the marriage lacks harmony, the line is faint. The ending of the line in a star indicates that the influence has ceased.

Marriage Line, Indications from

The Line of Marriage cuts the percussion horizontally between the Line of Heart and the Mount of Mercury.

Broken—separation or divorce.
Terminating at the Line of Apollo—rich marriage.
Forked at the start—separation due to one's own fault.
Close to the Line of Heart—marriage between 18 and 21.
Curving upwards—no marriage at all.
Sloping towards the Line of Heart—widowhood.
Black spots—domestic troubles.
The longer the line, the longer the union.

Marriage, Lines of

The Lines of Affection, more commonly known as Marriage Lines, appear on the side of the hand just below the little finger and just above the Heart Line. They sometimes run as far inward as the Mount of Mercury, under the little finger. These lines always relate to the opposite sex and never to the blood relation.

"Every Affection Line upon the hand does not necessarily represent marriage but it does represent an affection that you have felt or will feel for someone."

—*Frances Kienzle*

Marriage, Love

Branch from the Line of Fate merging into the Line of Heart.
Branch from the Mount of Moon merging with the Line of Fate.
Cross on the Mount of Jupiter.
Long fine Line of Marriage.

Marriage Mismated

Branch from the Line of Fate cutting the Line of Heart.
Deep bar cutting the Line of Heart.

Line of influence from the Mount of Moon or Mars cutting the Line of Fate.
Broken Line of Heart.
Poor Line of Fate.
Branch from the Line of Heart ending in a crook on the Mount of Saturn.

Marriage Troubles

The Line of Marriage crossed by many perpendicular lines.

Marriage, Unfit for

When in a man's hand the finger of Jupiter is short and crooked, the first phalange of the thumb heavy, and the second phalange poor, the lower mounts overdeveloped, the Heart Line short and without branches, it will be well not to marry that person. He is passionate, tyrannical, has no sense of honour or duty, and selfishness is the ruling passion of his life.

– E. Rene

Marriage, Wealthy

A cross and a star on the Mount of Jupiter.

Marriage with an Artist

A branch from the Line of Marriage upwards on the Mount of Sun or Apollo.

Marriage with an Old Person

A line from the Rascette to the Mount of Venus and thence to the Mount of Saturn.

Marriage with a Trader

A line from the Rascette to the Mount of Venus and thence to the Mount of Mercury.

Mars, the Line of

The Line of Mars is the sister line of the Line of Life. It runs inside the semicircle of the Life Line and parallel to it. Starting from the Mount of Mars, it adds to the qualities of the Line of Life.

A deep and well-cut Line of Mars covers up the defects of the Line of Life if it is thin, broad, shallow or chained. If both the lines are deep, the subject is characterized with high vitality, aggression and resistance. Black or red hair will further intensify these elements.

Martian Type

A person with the Mount of Mars predominant is called the Martian. He is aggressive by nature. He has offensive and defensive qualities of an extreme kind. He loves fight for its own sake. Peaceful life does not attract him. He loves all the material things that are within his reach. He spreads about the peacock feathers of vitality and wealth to attract the opposite sex.

Material Love

The Line of Heart starting from under the Mount of Saturn.

A strong Mount of Venus.

Maternity, Danger of

A line from the upper part of the Mount of Venus to the Mount of Saturn.

Mathematician's Hand

Love for Higher Mathematics is indicated by:
   Mounts of Sun and Moon absent.

Very straight Line of Head.
Second phalanges of fingers and thumb above normal.
Mounts of Saturn and Mercury predominant
The fourth finger above normal.
Fingers long and knotted.
Dry hard palm.

Meanness

Very narrow Quadrangle.
Line of Heart curving towards the Line of Head.
Fingers close together.
Fingers bent forward.
Thin hard palm.

Measurements

I have to call your attention to the fact that the measurements on the Line of Fate are modified by the length of the hand, while measurements on the Line of Life are mostly influenced by the breadth of the hand.

—*Comte C. de Saint-Germain*

Mechanical Aptitude

Ability for mechanical parts of fine arts is shown by:
Straight Line of Head.
Mount of Mercury thrown towards the Mount of Sun.
Palm longer than fingers.
Fingers with square tips.
Second knots of fingers marked.

Mechanical Powers

A square hand with spatulate fingers shows good mechanical powers. "The finest useful mechanism has

THE DICTIONARY OF PALMISTRY 163

been turned out by men with the square hand and the spatulate fingers."

Medical Profession

A judicious study of Palmistry would also afford assistance to the medical profession in diagnosing cases or in tracing hereditary traits, tendencies and characteristics. Doctors do sometimes examine the hands in certain ailments, but a closer attention to the subject would yield much useful information not always possible to obtain from the patient by other means.

—E. Rene

Medical Stigmata

Four to seven clear downward lines on the Mount of Mercury denote the scientist, especially the physician or surgeon.

—Comte C. de Saint-Germain

Mediocrity

Lack of ambition in life is shown by:
Mount of Mars absent.
Low Plain of Mars.
Low Triangle.
Line of Head poor.
Line of Fate feeble.
Line of Sun absent.
Mounts insignificantly developed.
First finger below normal.
First phalanx of the thumb very short.
Soft hands:
Short fingers

Melancholia

Wavy drooping line on third phalanx of the second finger.

Drooping Line of Head.
No Mounts of Sun or Jupiter.
Exaggerated Mount of Saturn.
Mount of Saturn much lined.
A grille on the Mount of Moon.

Memory, Bad

Broken Line of Head.
Line of Liver wavy or fragmentary.

Memory, Good

Line of Head fine and straight.
Line of Liver excellent.
First and fourth fingers conical.

Memory, Loss of

The Line of Head broken, giving the appearance of squares.

Mercenary Mental Make-Up

Mercenary spirit in social, intellectual and artistic work is indicated by:
Line of Sun terminating on the Mount of Mercury.
Mount of Moon insignificant.
Line of Head very straight and stiff.
Third finger too short.
Third finger leaning towards fourth.
Square-tipped fingers.
Hard palm.

Mercenary Soldier

One with the Mount of Mercury leaning towards the Upper Mount of Mars will turn out to be a mercenary soldier.

Mercurian Type

A person with the Mount of Mercury predominant is called the Mercurian. He is very shrewd in business affairs. He loves big schemes and big enterprises. Small business does not interest him. He is gifted with an unusual tact. He brings all his resources into play to accomplish certain ends. He loves travel and change of scene.

Mercury, Line of

Sometimes the Line of Mercury acts as the Line of Apollo or Saturn in the latter's absence. If the Line of Mercury is very short, in all probability it is not a Mercury but a chance line. In all cases the Line of Mercury runs towards the Mount of Mercury even though it may not actually reach it. In no case does it run towards any other Mount.

Mercury, Qualities of the Mount of

Normal—Occultist, eloquent, inventor, discoverer.
Above Normal—dreamer of a better world, inventor, dangerous schemer, unscrupulous adventurer.
Below Normal—Fine thoughts badly blended, handicapped eloquence, uncreativeness, unprofitable activity.

Military Honours

A star or triangle on either Mount of Mars.
A triangle between the lines of Life and Fate.

Military Mind

One deep line on third phalanx of second finger.
Triangle on Upper Mount of Mars.
Triangle in the Plain of Mars.
Three chief lines only (Life, Head, Heart) present.
Strong Mounts of Venus and Jupiter.

Palm longer than fingers
Fingers with square tips.
Mounts and the Plain of Mars predominant.

Misanthrope

Short Line of Heart.
Mounts of Sun and Venus absent.
Pronounced Mount of Saturn.
Mount of Saturn badly marked.
Long, knotty spatulate fingers.

Miserly Mind

A very narrow Quadrangle.
Heart Line often absent.
Line of Head cutting hand like a bar.
Hand thin and hard.
Thumb close to first finger.
Fingers bent inward.

Mixed Hand

These hands are mixed varieties of one or more types. "Without these hands, that is to say,'without the mixed intelligence peculiar to them", says d'Arpentigny, "society, deprived of its lights and shades, and without normal alkalies to effect the combination of its acids, and to amalgamate and modify them, world would advance only by struggles and leaps."

Moodiness

People with yellow hands are moody, moony and melancholy. They are plagued by the blues and cross the bridges without reaching them. They are irritable and unhappy, eating into themselves.

Moon, Qualities of the Mount of

Normal—Imagination of higher order, the gifted artist, healthy love of poetry love of nature.

Above Normal—Sheer madness, absence of commonsense, violent mental derangement.

Below Normal—Humdrum existence, imitative life, no thought of the future.

Moons on the Nails

Large moons always denote strong action of the heart and rapid circulation of blood, but when unusually large they indicate too much pressure on the heart, rapidity in its beat, the valves are overstrained and the danger of bursting some blood vessel in the heart or in the brain. Small moons indicate the reverse of this. They always denote poor circulation, weak action of the heart and anaemia of the brain. When close to death the moons are the first to take on a bluish look and later on the entire nail becomes blue or almost black in colour.

—*Cheiro*

Moral Depravity

Line of Head drooping.
Line of Head forked.
Line of Heart forkless.
Heart Line starting under the Mount of Saturn.
Double or triple Girdle of Venus.
Mount of Venus cross-rayed.
Mounts of Mercury and Moon dominant.
Mounts of Jupiter and Sun insignificant.
Thin hands with long fingers.

Morbid Disposition

Line of Liver wavy.
Line of Liver fragmentary.
Line of Head drooping into the Mount of Moon.
Mount of Moon much rayed.
Palm soft and yellow-hued.

Second finger very long.
Mount of Saturn exaggerated.
Mount of Saturn covered with confused lines.
Lines yellow and weak.
Third finger shorter than second finger.

Morbidness. Oversensitive

If the cushion-like formations on the inside of the finger-tips and thumbs are over-developed, these indicate over-sensitiveness to the point of morbidness.

Mounts, Location of

The Mounts are the fleshy cushions that lie at the base of fingers, under the thumb, and on either side of the hand, making seven in number.
Mount of Jupiter—beneath the forefinger.
Mount of Saturn—at the base of the second finger
Mount of Sun or Apollo—under the third finger.
Mount of Mercury—under the little finger.
Mount of Venus—at the base of the thumb.
Mount of Moon—located on the lower outside part of the hand.
Upper Mount of Mars—between thumb and forefinger.
Lower Mount of Mars—between little finger and the Mount of Moon.

Mounts, Meaning of

Mounts are elevations of skin in the palm, mostly below the fingers. These indicate the following qualities:
Jupiter—Political ambition and power.
Saturn—Reserve, melancholy, seriousness.
Sun or Apollo—brilliancy, fruitfulness success.
Mercury—Science and commerce.
Venus—love and passion.

Mars—Vitality, courage, warlike spirit.
Moon—Fickleness, romance and imagination.

Mount, Presence of

A mount is considered present and active, although it be not marked by any rising, if it is marked by lines and signs.

—*Comte C. de Saint-Germain*

Mount Type

The palm constitutes five-tenths of the inner surface. In greater or lesser proportion the Mounts occupy space, to this degree the man is said to belong to a Mount Type.

—*Alice Denton Jennings*

Much-Ado-About-Nothing Mentality

The mind of a man who is very busy doing nothing of real worth is indicated by:
Exaggerated first phalanx of the thumb.
Head Line crossing the hand like a bar.
Exaggerated Mount of Mars.
Hand much rayed.
Fingers with spatulate tips.
Palm longer than fingers.

Murderer for Profit

The Line of Head heavily marked.
The Line of Head with a decided growth upwards.
The Line of Head rising high towards Mercury.
The hand unusually hard.
The thumb abnormally thick, long and stiff.

Murderer, The Slow

Short Line of Life.
Line of Head drooping.

Mount of Moon much rayed.
Mount of Mercury marked with cross lines.
Mount of Sun exaggerated.
Stars on the second finger.
The Mount of Moon much rayed.
Knotty fingers.
Long thin hands.

Murderer, Treacherous

Thin, hard hand.
Long fingers, slightly curved inward.
Thumb long with both phalanges well-developed.
The Line of Head set high across the hand.
The Line of Head long and thin.
The Mount of Venus depressed.
Such are the hands of the skilled artists in crime. Murder with such persons is reduced to a fine art, in the execution of which they study every detail. They will rarely, if ever, kill their victim by violence—such a thing will be vulgar in their eyes—poison is the chief instrument that they employ, but so skilfully that the verdict is usually 'Death from natural causes.'

—*Cheiro*

Murderer, Very Habitual

The Line of Head short, thick and red.
The nails short and red.
The hand heavy and coarse.
The thumb set very low.
The thumb short and thick in the second phalanx.
The first phalanx of the thumb "club-shaped"—short, broad and square.
Mount of Venus—abnormally large.

Murderer, Violent

Large cross in the Triangle.

Stars on the second finger.
Lines of Head and Heart short.
Exaggerated Mounts of Mars and Venus.
Thick hard hands.
Spatulate fingers.
Clubbed thumb
Main lines very red.

Musical Genius

The Circle of Musical Genius is found between the third and fourth finger. It is a sign of supreme brilliancy in the field of music.

Musical Instrumentalists

Palm shorter than fingers.
Fingers with square tips.
Second knot on fingers.
Strong Mount of Mercury.
Line of Head separated from the Line of Life.

Musical Man

Great aptitude for music is shown by:
Hands soft and conical.
Fingers smooth.
Mounts of Sun, Moon and Venus well-developed
Line of Head drooping.

Musician's Hand

Spatulate or square fingers.
Mount of Venus firm.
High Mount of Venus.
Angles of music on the outside of the thumb

Mystic Cross

A cross on the Quadrangle shows great interest in occult and hidden sciences, clairvoyance, etc. Therefore, it is known as the Mystic Cross.

N

Nails

Scientists think that nails are formed by the electric fluids inside the body. These are hardened by exposure to the air, thus becoming a kind of intervenery substance between the electric fluid and the human skin and flesh.

—Martini

Nails, Good

Good nails are glossy and white, slightly pink, not brittle, transparent, long, normal, and not too thin. This is an indication of good spirit and refinement.

Nails, Indications from

Microscopically considered, the nails are composed of hair-like fibres. Closely knit together these form a compact hornlike substance and shield the concentration of nerve-filaments under them.

Short nails—criticism and inquisitiveness.
Short and hard—quarrelsomeness.
Short nails with a soft palm—inborn critic.
Short and pale—deceitful disposition.
Short and red—violent temper.
Short, square and bluish—heart trouble.
Short and triangular—paralysis.
Short, curved and narrow—spinal trouble.
Broad, long and round—sound judgment.
Thin, long and brittle—weak constitution.
Thin, long and narrow—timidity.
White spots on nails—bad circulation of blood.
Nails of the first phalanx bent inward—scrofula and consumption.

Ridges—single-mindedness.
Cross ridges—signs of disease.

Nails, Qualities of

The long-nailed people are more idealistic and less critical. Short-nailed people are observant of the smallest details.

Nails, Perfect

Perfect nails are naturally brilliant, white and almond-shaped. These declare happy nature and roseate health.

Napoleon's Index

When first finger is equal to the second, it is called "Napoleon's Index". It is an indication of great political ambition, military glory and boundless love of wealth and power.

Naval Profession

Large knotty fingers.
A large Mount of Moon.
Mount of Moon much lined.
Fine Mounts and Plain of Mars.
Large first phalanx of the thumb.
Line of Head drooping.
Line of Head separated from the Line of Life at the start.

Negative Existence

A total absence of the mounts indicates a negative existence. It means that the subject did not have a chance to develop his character.

Nervous Trouble

Branches rising from a black spot on the Line of Life.

Neuralgia

Nervous troubles and disorders are indicated by:
  Black spot on the Line of Life.
  Line of Life chained.
  Spot or dot on the Mount of Moon.
  Mount of Saturn exaggerated.
  Mount of Saturn much lined.
  Flat first phalanx of the thumb.
  Plain of Mars hollow towards the Moon.
  Mount of Moon much rayed.
  Mount of Moon predominant.
  Deep colourless identations on the Line of Head
  Island on the Line of Head.

Nurse

Indications of a good nurse are:
  No worry lines.
  Lines of Head and Heart healthy.
  Fine Mounts of Jupiter and Venus
  Fine Mount of Mercury.
  Medical Stigmata.
  Elastic palm.
  Long knotty fingers.
  Smooth joints.
  A small thumb.
  A grille on the Mount of Moon.
  Two clear-cut vertical lines on the fourth finger.

O

Observation, Importance of

The greatest truth may lie in smallest things,
The greatest good in what we most despise,
The greatest light may break from darkest skies,
The greatest chord from even the weakest strings

—Cheiro

Obstinacy

Mounts of Mars exaggerated.
Line of Head starting from under the Mount of Saturn.
Line of Head rather short.
Hard palm.
Spatulate or square fingers.
First knot marked.
Short broad nails.
Short but flat first phalanx of the thumb.

Occult Sciences, Aptitude for

Mounts of Moon, Mercury and Saturn predominant.
Thin palm.
Long smooth fingers.
Drooping Line of Head.
The small triangle well-formed.
Triangle on the Mount of Moon.
A cross in the Quadrangle.
Line of Intuition.

Officiousness

Very large hands show a harmful mania for useless details.
Such a person is meddlesome and officious.

Old Age

The outcome of career is indicated by the termination of the Fate Line. If it is deep and well-cut, it is expressive of a prosperous old age. If it is broken, old age will be weary and worried. A tasselled end indicates financial difficulties in old age.

Opera Singer

Palm larger than fingers.
Fingers with conical tips.
Lines of Life and Heart widely separated at the start.
Line of Head forked at the termination

Opposite Sex, Influence of

A star on the Mount of Venus.
Line descending from the Line of Heart to the Line of Head without reaching it.

Optimistic Hand-Reading

To take away hope is to take away life. A doctor does not allow his patient to know the fears he has of his ultimate recovery, but tells him he will get well, and often to the amazement of the physician the sick man does recover. In the same way fix the idea in a man's mind that he can and will succeed and it will go a long way towards rendering him successful, and the palmist can point out the most favourable course to purpose, or the talent that will best repay cultivation.

—*E. Rene*

Ordinary Illness

The Line of Life cut by a number of small lines.

Organic Affection

Organic affection is indicated by livid holes upon any line.

Origin of Palmistry

Modern Palmistry owes its origin to ancient Hindus. The Egyptian priests and Chaldean shepherds added to the rich Hindu lore. Pythagoras and Aristotle also made significant researches in the science and art of Palmistry. The Arabian alchemists, the European astrologers, the German philosophers, the French scientists and the English savants, have all contributed to the investigations of Palmistry.

It is widely accepted internationally that Hindus were the originators of Palmistry. The scientific knowledge of ancient Hindus was quite astonishing. For instance, without any scientific instruments, the ancient Hindu sages determined the precision of the Equinox to take place once in 25,850 years. Modern astronomers accept this as correct.

Other People, Influence of

The more numerous the Lines of Influence, the greater is the number of people who have become a part of the subject's life. The lesser the number, the more self-contained is the individual.

Overdoing Luck

When the Line of Fate runs beyond the palm, cutting into the Finger of Saturn it is not a good sign, as everything will go too far. As a leader, his followers will go beyond his wishes. They will probably turn back and attack the commander, as it happened to Columbus.

Overindulgence

Overindulgence in sexual matters is indicated if the

hand is sensual, Mount of Venus large with strong Lines of Life and Mars.

Overworked Intellect

An overworked intellect is indicated by a frayed Line of Head.

P

Painter

A successful painter is indicated by:
Conically tipped fingers.
Strong Mount of Venus.
Mount of Sun excellent.
Strong Mount of Moon.
Drooping Line of Head.
Soft hands.

Palmist

"Confide in me", the Palmist said;
And then my hand glanced over,
And told me when I was to wed
With my brave soldier lover;
He told me of riches and of long life—
Of joy I would discover;
And now I know he told me true—
I've wed my soldier lover.

—*Anonymous*

Palmist, Qualities of

The more intellect, refinement, tact, and facility of expression you have, the more you can accomplish. The greater your knowledge of life in all its phases, the more skilful you will be. All can acquire by study a certain degree of proficiency; those who are best endowed mentally, and are also the best reasoners, will become the best practitioners.

Palmistry

Palmistry is a science, which in its highest and truest

conception has for its aim the motto of the ancients; 'Know Thyself', the simplest and grandest sermon that can ring in human ears

—*Alice Denton Jennings*

Thus, in arming yourself with this science, you arm yourself with a great power and you will have a thread that will guide you into the labyrinth of the most impenetrable hearts.

—*Balzac*
Le Cousin Pons

Since the beginning of history, man has been intrigued by the lines in his hands. And throughout the ages students of Palmistry through observation, experiment, comparison and analogy have worked out the noteworthy science of hand-reading.

—*Frances Kienzle*

Palmistry, Chiromancy, Chirosophy—call it what you like—has been said to trace its mysteries to the stars, their influence on the earth and its denizens, the magnetic fluid that incontestably issues from their faraway splendour.

—*Comte C. de Saint-Germain*

Palm, Qualities of

Narrow Palm—lack of courage, joy, imagination.
Wide palm—strong health.
Thick and too wide—violent temper.
Flat and high palm—great pride.
Very hollow palm—domestic trouble.

Palpitation of the Heart

The Line of Liver red at the start.

Paralysis

Main lines poorly marked.
Grille or star on the Mount of Moon.
Star on the Mount of Saturn.
Mount of Saturn much lined.
Nails short and triangular in shape.

Passionate Crime

Black spots on the thumb indicate a crime caused by passion.

Perseverance

Mount of Mercury well-developed.
Fourth finger excellent.
Long, straight Line of Head.
Lower Mount of Mars predominant.
Strong first phalanx of the thumb.
Elastic palm.
Square knotted fingers.

Personal Magnetism

"A hand warmer than normal (almost hot) indicates personal magnetism, vivacity, also a hasty temper."

Pessimism, Literary

If the Mount of Saturn leans towards the Mount of Sun, it indicates that the subject can become another Thomas Hardy, Shelley or Keats, sublimating his pessimism into a literary exposition of brilliance.

Pets, Love for

Love for pets is indicated by the Mount of Apollo leaning towards the Mount of Saturn.

Philosophic Knot

On the first finger there is a prominence outside the

topmost joint. This is known as the philosophic knot and shows a desire for information and enquiry. Such people love mystery in all things. They discard the dramatic clash and colour of life for the visionary similes and vapourish drapings of the spirit. Theirs is the peace of the aesthetic. Their domain is beyond the borderland of matter. They enjoy the cloudland of thought. They have no love for the dreaded grub-worm of materialism.

Philosopher

The philosophers have angular hands, generally long with bony fingers, well-developed joints and rather long nails. They study mankind. They know every chord and tone in the harp of life. They play upon it. They are gratified with its responsive melody more than the click of the coin. Aptitude for the study of Philosophy is indicated by:

Very long knotted fingers.
Thin hard palm.
Fingers spatulate.
Finger tips conical.
Good Lines of Head and Heart.

Physician

Square-tipped knotted fingers.
Medical Stigmata on the Mount of Mercury.
Good Head Line.
First knot on all the fingers.
Long fingers.
Science lines on Mercury.
Good Mount of Venus.
Luna well-shaped.

Pickpocket

Poor drooping Line of Head.

Mount of Moon exaggerated.
An exaggerate Mount of Mercury.
Mount of Mercury much lined.
Thin, narrow palm.
Long, thin crooked fingers.

Pictures, Palmistry in

In an old book written in Sanskrit in my possession the meanings given to lines on the palm are worked out in pictures. At the end of what we call the Line of Life appears the design of an elephant indicating that line reaching this portion of the hand promised extreme long life, the elephant being an animal which can live to an enormous age.

—*Cheiro*

Pleurisy

A line rising from the Line of Life ending in an island on the Mount of Saturn.

Poetical Power

Pointed fingers.
Line of Heart chained.
Line of Fate islanded.
Drooping Line of Head.
Mounts of Sun, Moon and Venus prominent.
Thin, soft palm.
Long, thin first phalanx of the thumb.

Pointed Angle

If the lines of Head and Heart part at a pointed angle, it expresses the subject's sensitive nature. The more pointed the angle, the more sensitive he is. He will never think of causing hurt to anybody even if it amounts to the hampering of his own interests.

Politician

The Line of Head drooping.
Upper Mount of Mars much-lined.
Exaggerated Mount of Jupiter.
Mount of Mercury insignificant.
Mount of Mercury badly marked.

Poverty

A branch from the Line of Head reaching the Mount of Jupiter with a cross at its tip.
A crescent at the root of the Ring Finger.
Star on the Mount of Saturn.
The Great Triangle intercepted by two wavy lines giving the appearance of a cross.
Faint and broken Rascettes.
Low Mount of Mercury.
Life Line ending with a cross.
A faint, wavy or broken Fate Line.
Fate Line reaching the bottom phalanx of Saturn finger.
Cross attached to the Line of Life.

Predetermination

Palmists can only foresee coming events when the factors of these exist in the individual character or are set in motion by present influences, circumstances, and environment, but these laws being by no means immutable, there is always hope of escape from impending disaster. Favourable forecasts must not be looked upon as infallible, otherwise disappointments may result.

—*E. Rene*

Prediction about Life

I have always made a practice of never predicting length of life by the lines in the hands. Different types of people would react differently to such predictions. Some types would not be perturbed at all, while a highly nervous person might be terribly upset

—*Frances Kienzle*

Pride, Indomitable

Exaggerated Mount of Sun.
Exaggerated Mount of Jupiter.
Exaggerated Mounts and Plain of Mars.
Grille on the Mount of Jupiter.
Branches from Lines of Life and Head running high up into the Mount of Jupiter.

Priesthood

Cross in the Quadrangle under the Mount of Saturn.
Good lines of Head and Heart.
Mount of Venus moderate.
Short nails.
Pointed first finger.
A good Apollo finger.
Long fingers.
Conic finger of Jupiter.
First phalanx of Mercury long.
Mount of Venus good.
Luna developed.
Straight Jupiter finger.

Prints of Hands

Place a small wad of cotton under the sheet of paper about where the hollow of the palm would rest. Spread the ink evenly and lightly over the palm. Preferably use printer's ink. Spread the fingers widely apart on the paper to get clear impressions. Before lifting the hand from the paper, give it a slightly rolling movement on the side in order to print the lines on the side of the hand. Be sure to write the name and the date of print.

Prison Life

Grille on the Mount of Saturn.
Square on the Mount of Venus

Profession Choice of

There is no doubt that this science is of eminently practical value in the choice of vocation. Mistakes of young people in entering upon a calling for which they have no natural ability or disposition are frequently dearly paid for later in life. There is no need of a blind choice, as a scientific analysis of characteristics of their mental and physical make-up is disclosed, among other factors, by the formation of lines of their hands, and can point the way to the calling they are most suitable for.

—*Josef Ranald*

Profligacy

A complete and full Girdle of Venus indicates profligacy of the worst type. The children having this sign must be properly watched and carefully brought up.

Prophet-Mongering

A wise man will listen to the advice of the prophet, accept the encouragement it gives, and follow it only in so far as it accords with reason and good judgment.

—*E. Rene*

Prostration, Nervous

Wide and long nails with bluish tint.

Prudence

Fine Lower Mount of Mars.
Mount of Mercury well-developed.
Fourth finger slightly above average.
Lines of Life and Head joined for some distance at the start.
Finger tips square.
Second knots marked.
Second phalanx of the thumb above normal.
Fine second finger.
Mount of Saturn well formed.

Psychic Hand

The psychic people have almond-shaped hands. These are long, narrow and fragile-looking hands. They have slender tapering fingers and long almond-shaped nails. The psychics have idealistic natures. They are visionaries. They are of a spiritual bent of mind and appreciate a search for truth.

"They are the lilies", says Cheiro, "thrown, by some ruthless hand, upon the tempest-tossed river of life. They seem so helpless in the forward sweep of the terrible current. One sees them at times clinging to the banks for pity. Ah! those beautiful hands have no strength; they are swept on again by the rising tide of bubbling frothy humanity."

Psychology of Hand

The psychology of hand is, like medicine, an art as well as science, and accordingly intuition plays a part in it. But intuition must not be confused by clairvoyance.... Modern psychology is based on experiment and statistics and includes within its purview the investigation of physical signs and their correlations with personality. Carus, Vaschide and I have shown that the hand contains a great number of such signs that contribute to the interpretation of personality.

—*Charlott Wolfe*
THE HUMAN HAND

Public Honours

A triangle on the Mount of Mercury.
A star on the first joint of the first finger.
A star on the Mount of Jupiter.

Quadrangle

The principal lines trace two figures on the hand. The upper figure is called the Quadrangle and the lower figure is called the Triangle. The Quadrangle is also called the Table of the Hand. It is an horizontal elongated figure, stretching itself clear across the hand between the Lines of Heart and Head. A wide Quadrangle denotes broad-mindedness. A narrow Quadrangle indicates narrow-mindedness.

R

Rashness

Lines of Head and Life widely separated.
Exaggerated Mount of Jupiter.
Upper Mars well-developed.
Third finger abnormally long.

Rays of Influence

The Lines of Influence are the rays of influence. These create for us a sunshine of happiness or a moonshine of sorrow, usually as they go upwards or downwards respectively. These tell of other people who have left an impression on the mind of the subject.

Reading, Love of

First finger conical.
Fine Line of Head.
Head Line drooping.
Head Line and Life Line joined at the start.
Mount of Sun well-formed.
Mount of Venus prominent.

Reciprocated Affection

Reciprocated affection is indicated by white marks on the thumb.

Reflection

Knotty fingers arrest the impetuousness of disposition and give reflections.

—Cheiro

Relatives, Influence of

If a deep Line of Fate, rising inside the Life Line, ends on the Mount of Jupiter, it indicates spectacular success produced by a Jupiterean ambition on one hand and the influence of relatives on the other.

Relatives on the Line of Apollo

If the Line of Apollo is accompanied by influence lines from the Mount of Venus, relatives are largely responsible for the success of the subject. If the Line of Apollo is cut by a line branching from the Line of Heart, the relatives will stand as obstructions in his way.

Religion

It must be stated, and stated clearly, that the hand does not recognise the mere fact of ceremony, be it civil or religious. It merely registers the influence of different people over our lives.

—*Cheiro*

Reverses of Fortune

A cross on the Mount of Sun indicates reverses of fortune.

Rheumatism

"Satin skin."
A downward line from the Mount of Moon.
Exaggerated Mount of Saturn.
Mount of Saturn much lined.
Mount of Moon exaggerated.
Line of Life widely forked.
Line of Life red at the termination.
Cross lines from the Line of Life to the Mount of Saturn.

Robber, The Highway

The highwayman has the following indications:—
Star on the Mount of Mercury.

Grille on the Mount of Mercury.
Life, Head and Heart lines red in colour.
Minor lines missing.
Mount of Mars prominent.
Mount of Moon excellent.
Thick hard hand.
Soft smooth heavy fingers.

Romance

The railway of romance runs under the fourth finger, just below the Mount of Mercury. Those who entrain for marriage should survey the Line of Affection carefully lest they are jettisoned over the bridge of despondency.

Romantic Madness

As Shakespeare said:
"A lover, a poet, and madman.
Are of imagination all compact."
A romantically madman can be signalized by the following observations:—
Line of Heart drooping into the Mount of Moon.
A star on a branch of Heart Line
Star on the Mount of Moon.
Mount of Moon connected with the Mount of Venus through an influence line.

Romantic Nature

Line of Heart starting from the Mount of Saturn.
Drooping Line of Head.
Mount of Moon high.
Girdle of Venus quite distinct.
Mount of Venus well-developed.
Mount of Venus much rayed.
Hand spatulate.

Roseate Health

Line of Mars deeply marked.
Mount of Jupiter exaggerated.
Red Lines
Red nails.
Red skin.

Roosevelt, Hand of

Alice Denton Jennings makes the following observation about the hand of Mr. Franklin D. Roosevelt, one of the greatest presidents of U.S.A. :—

"The Fate Line, starting as it does, low on the Mount of Moon to the side of the hand, destined president Roosevelt to lead a public life. This line, traversing the hand, as it does in a straight unbroken line, denotes his unusual and outstanding public success."

S

Sadness, Imaginary

Second finger leaning towards the first.
Exaggerated second finger.
Exaggerated Mount of Saturn
Drooping Line of Head
Exaggerated Mount of Moon.

Satin Skin

"Satin skin" means extra-smooth skin of the palm. It is a tendency to rheumatism and gout.

Saturnian Type

A person with the Mount of Saturn predominant is called the Saturnian. He is habitually reserved, a profound thinker, a born recluse, and a confirmed cynic. He is the born doubter of everything in the world. He is the "balance wheel" of all types. His character is a check against impulsiveness. Agriculture comes home to him. He likes the sad and serious things of life. He studies sciences without recreation. You cannot please him, because for him sadness is a kind of recreation.

Saturn, line of

The Line of Fate is also called the Line of Saturn, because it usually runs from the Rascette to the Mount of Saturn.

Saturn, Qualities of the Mount

Normal—Poetic sadness, morbidness, love of loneliness, love of agriculture.
Above Normal—Morbid melancholy, Pessimism, hatred of mankind.

Below Normal—Realism in art, disbelief in **ghosts**, reasonless indifference, unsocial drudgery.

Saturn, The Ring of

Rising between the fingers of Saturn and Jupiter, the Ring of Saturn encircles the finger of Saturn and terminates between the fingers of Saturn and Apollo.

The Ring of Saturn is very seldom found and it is not a good sign to have. Its presence is indicative of a shifting and vacillating character. He is unable to concentrate his efforts on anything. He changes his professions hurriedly without achieving any measure of success.

"The Ring of Saturn is a mark very seldom found and is not a good sign to have it on the hand. I have closely watched people possessing it, and I have never yet observed that they were in any way successful. It seems to cut off the Mount of Saturn in such a way that such people never gain any point that they may work for or desire."

—*Cheiro*

Scandal

A Line of influence cutting the Line of Apollo and terminating in an island denotes disgrace and public scandal due to guilty intrigues.

Scarlet Fever

A small square on the Line of Life with an upright cross inside denotes scarlet fever.

Scholar's Hand

Good Head Line.
Good Mount of Luna.
Short nails for criticism.
A long first phalanx of Mercury.

Well-developed conic finger of Jupiter.

Science and Art Combined

The Mount of Sun projecting towards the Mount of Mercury.
Second knot of fingers.
Finger-tips square.
A triangle on the Mount of Sun.
Line of Sun ending on the Mount of Mercury.
Line of Sun ending between third and fourth finger.
"Often", says Comte C. de Saint-Germain, "a Line of Sun is triple-forked at the termination, throwing a prong towards the Mount of Mercury and one towards the Mount of Saturn."

Science of Palmistry

Palmistry is not a science in the strictly scientific sense of the word. It is not a science like Chemistry and Physics which are presumed to be mathematically correct, even though their reasonings are rapidly changing and the soundest theories of yesterday are exploded today. Palmistry is a science, because it is based on systematic study of the hand. It is a science in the same sense as Psychology, Civics, Political Science, Economics and other social sciences.

As Stansfield Sargent puts it, "Astronomy, Chemistry and Physics are readily recognised as sciences. They involve careful laboratory work, exact measurement, rigid laws and sure-fire practicability. Psychology is concerned with something less definite and tangible. exactitude is hard and exceptionless laws almost never occur." The same is true of Palmistry.

"There is no mystery about Palmistry. It is a science, pure and simple."

—*Frances Kienzle*

"The science of Palmistry is founded upon the shape

of the hand. It is by the development of what are known as the Mounts, seven in number, which lie at the base of fingers, and along the sides of the hand, by estimating properly their various combinations, that we are able accurately to delineate the character of any subject presented to us."

—*William G. Benham*

"If you were in a plane flying over a fast express train, you could look down and see it travelling. You could also, from your distance, look ahead and see that around a curve a bridge has been washed out. You know that in a matter of seconds the train would crash and all the occupants would probably be killed instantly, or at least seriously injured. The people on the train would be blissfully innocent. In that incident you would be looking into space. Palm-reading is much the same. You look at the dangers ahead and guard against them. But if you don't know what to look for, then you are like the people in the train."

—*Frances Kienzle*

Science, Success in

Fourth finger as long as the second.
A triangle on the Line of Head.
White dots on the Line of Head.

Aptitude for research is indicated by:
The Medical Stigmata on the Mount of Mercury.
Thin hands.
Long knotted fingers.
Mount of Saturn finely-shaped and prominent.
Second finger well-developed.

Scientific Genius

Scientific genius is indicated by three little lines (also called Medical Stigmata) at the base of the third finger. It shows a keen analytical mind and an intellectual brilliance for scientific research.

A triangle on the Line of Head close to the Mount of Mercury shows success in the matters of scientific research.

Sculptor

A successful sculptor is indicated by:
Square-tipped fingers.
Mount of Sun well-developed.
Mount of Venus strong.
Strong Mount of Moon.
Head Line drooping slightly.
Soft hands.

Second Finger, Qualities of

Too short—indulgence.
Too long—morbidity.
Crooked—murderer's instinct.
Fair size—prudence.
Leaning towards the first finger—whimsical depression.
Leaning towards the third finger—morbidity.
Longer than the first—morbid foolishness.
Equal to the first finger—ambition.
Shorter than the first finger—ambition.
Longer than the third finger—mania for greatness.
Equal to the third finger—gambling instinct.
Shorter than the third finger—foolhardy enterprises.

Seers, Sages and Saints

Line of Intuition.
Mystic cross.
High Mount of Moon.
Pointed smooth fingers.
Transparent hand.

Almond-shaped nails.

Self-Abuse

The Girdle of Venus is dangerous to the adolescents who must be properly guarded against wasting their energies by self-abuse. The mind is inflamed and full of imagination about lascivious dreams. This makes him a lover of solitude. He must be drawn into the sparkle of society to cure him of the unhealthy practice.

Self-Confidence

If the Head Line is separated from the Heart Line at the commencement, it shows onfidence in one's ability and disregard for the opinion of others.

Self-Contained Individual

When a person keeps the fingers of his hand partially closed, it shows a self-contained in lividual, cautious but trustworthy.

Self-Importance

When palm is held upward, finger closing loosely, the subject is full of self-importance.

Selfishness, Excessive

Hand thick and flabby.
Line of Heart absent.
Exaggerated Mounts of Venus and M on.
Short, smooth fingers.
Thick third phalanges.
Very pale palm and lines.

Self-Made Man

Fortune by unaided effort is indicated by:
  Branches of the Line of Fate ending o the Mount of Sun or Mercury.

Lines of Fate and Sun starting from inside the Triangle.
Long first phalanx of the thumb.
Fine, straight Line of Head.
Mounts of Sun and Mercury predominant.
Mounts of Mars well-marked.

Self-Projection

A whorl on the Lower Mount of Mars gives one prescience and the ability to project oneself into others without much effort.

Self-Reform

One of the great beauties of Palmistry is that one can see his own shortcomings and correct them.

—Frances Kienzle

Sensitiveness

Great sensitiveness of spirit is indicated by wedge-shaped nails.

Sensitiveness to Criticism

Many worry lines.
Exaggerated Mounts of Sun and Moon.
Lines of Life and Head attached a pretty distance.
Nails almond-shaped.
Short nails on second finger.

Sensuality

Boundless sensuality is indicated by the Mount of Venus leaning towards the Mount of Moon.

The semi-circular line, popularly known as the Girdle of Venus, is often characterized as indication of gross sensuality and relates more to the psychological side of Venus than just physical sensuality. It is not always a sign of intense licentiousness and unchastity. The subject has tendencies of debauchery and profligacy due to intense physical nervousness. Such a person is highly sensitive and touchy, taking home any slight or indifference. Thus he develops a pessimistic outlook, unable to find his own place in society. Thus he is likely to become a victim of hysteria.

A person with a Girdle of Venus, exhibiting no nervousness or hysteria, is likely to be very sensual, licentious and amorous, because the Girdle of Venus adds heat to his already warm character.

Sex Sublimation

The absence of the lines on the Mount of Venus shows an absence of electrifying currents, and this calm mount expends its energy in a love of beauty, gaiety, colour, art and dress, instead of the sexual desires.

—*William G. Benham*

Sign of Death

To have yellow speckles in the nails of one's hands is a great sign of death.

—*Milton*

Sister Life-Line

In some hands there are two life lines alongside. This extra line is called, "Sister Life Line". It shows that the possessor has great recuperative power. It adds strength to the Life Line.

Sister Lines

When a main line is accompanied by a sister line running alongside, it strengthens the main line. Any break in the main line is bridged over by the sister line

Sixth Sense

A whorl under the third finger gives a person the power to understand things which are not visible to the view. Such a person can succeed in any walk of life.

Size of the Hands

Very small hands—disorder of ideas.
Small hands—delicacy of mind.
Average hands—sound commonsense.
Large hands—love of details.
Very large hands—meddlesomeness.

Skill in Love

A line starting from the Mount of Venus and going up to the Mount of Mercury.

Skin, Climate of

Dry skin—tendency to fever.
Damp skin—serious liver trouble and ill-balanced moral nature.

Slippery Fellow

Rubbing hands together as if washing them indicates a slippery fellow. You cannot depend on him, because he is untruthful and hypocritical.

Smartness

Smartness and agility of mind is shown by:
  Long Line of Head.
  Strong first phalanx of the Thumb.
  Well-developed Mounts of Mercury and Mars.
  Elastic hand.
  Square tips.
  Fingers longer than the palm.

Soldier's Hand

Mounts of Mars firm.
Short spatulate or square fingers.

Flat palm.
Thumb heavy.
Mercury developed.

Solomon, The Ring of

The Ring of Solomon is the strange mark of mysticism and occult. Such a possessor is an adept in the supernatural sciences.

The Ring of Solomon is a small line having its source between the fingers of Jupiter and Saturn. It ends near the start of the Life Line, thus giving the impression of a ring.

If the hand is crossed by many lines, the Ring of Solomon has a pronounced effect. It shows the great impressionist and emotionalist with a strong zest for psychology.

Somnambulism

When the Line of Intuition starts in an island, it denotes somnambulism and clairvoyance. Other signs:
> Island on the Line of Liver at the starting point.
> Cross in the Quadrangle.

Space Between Life and Head

Small space between the Lines of Life and Head gives splendid energy and self-confidence. This is a useful sign for barristers, actors and preachers. People with such a mark will do well to sleep on their decisions. They are inclined to be too hasty, and unnecessarily self-confident.

When the space is too wide, it denotes a foolhardiness and excessive self-confidence endangering success.

Space Signs

> Wide space between first and second finger—great independence of thought.

Wide space between third and fourth finger—great independence of action.

Spatulate Hand

The nailed phalanges of the hand present the appearance of more or less a flattened-out spatula. Large thumbs are natural to these hands. They are good colonizers. Their self-confidence is extreme. They are valiant. They are active and industrious. They have the power and the genius of Cyclops. In ancient days they dotted the earth with battlemented castles. They are leaders in arts of peace and war.

"These people wonder that God took six days to make the world—with the little power that they possess, they would revolutionize the world in a day."

—Cheiro

Speculator's Hand

A sloping Line of Head.
The third finger almost as long as the second.

Speculator, Successful

Talent for successful speculative business is shown by:

    Long Line of Head.
    Line of Head drooping at the termination.
    Line of Head separated from the Line of Life at the start.
    High Mounts of Jupiter and Sun.
    First phalanx of the thumb thrown backwards.
    Very flexible fingers.
    Third finger above normal.

Spendthrift Disposition

High Mounts of Jupiter and Sun.
Very flexible fingers.

Line of Head separated from the Line of Life.
Line of Head drooping towards the Mount of Moon.
No knots.

Spinal Trouble

Mount of Moon rayed or starred.
Drooping Line of Life.
Line of Life broken under the Mount of Saturn.
Line of Life starred.
A star on the Mount of Saturn.
Nails short, narrow and curved.

Spiritual Inclination

Fine Mount of Jupiter.
Slender soft palm.
Smooth pointed fingers.

Sportsmanship

Love for outdoor life and games is indicated by:
 Only three chief lines.
 Mounts very low.
 No worry lines.
 Large hard hand.
 Spatulate finger tips.
 Third finger longer than normal.
 Lines of Life and Heart separated at the start.

Square

A square is always a favourable sign. It is a sign of protection against any possible harm.

Square Hand

It has a square appearance as a whole and its finger-tips are also square. It has a large thumb knotty fingers and the palm too looks square. The square-handed people are practical with a yearning for social security.

The earth", says d'Arpentigny, "is pre-eminently their abode, they can see nothing beyond the social life of man; they know no more of the world of ideas than what the naked eye can know of the heaven."

Squares, Signs from

Found near a star—escape from danger.
On the Mount of Venus—escape from imprisonment.
Broken square—narrow escape from danger.
Square on broken line—neutralizes ill effects.

Star

A star is a worthy and valuable sign. Usually it is good; but sometimes it is a bad indication, depending upon the location.

A star speaks of added strength, causing both illumination and explosion. It invariably intensifies the qualities and the subject endowed with surplus strength is likely to abuse his qualities.

Star of Brilliant Intellect

The Star of Brilliant Intellect is found at the bottom of the palm underneath the fourth finger. It shows reasoning power and a brilliant imagination. This star is almost always found in the hands of great thinkers, philosophers and brilliant logicians. They devote their life to an eternal search for light and truth. They are generally considered as visionaries. As a matter of fact, their dreams of today do become the realities of tomorrow.

Star of Tragic Fate

The Star of Tragic Fate is found at the base of the second finger. It shows a person whose career will come to a tragic end. The Life Line, terminating in a cross, heightens the tragedy.

Star of Unusual Faculties

Stars of Unusual Faculties are found on the tips of the fingers. Helen Keller, the blind international leader, has these signs. They are witnesses of an acute sense of touch. Little wonder, Helen Keller can hear, see and read through her finger-tips. Struck incurably deaf, dumb and blind at the age of nineteen months, she has overcome all her handicaps. She is an author, lecturer, educationist and tourist. She visited India in 1955 at the invitation of Premier Nehru.

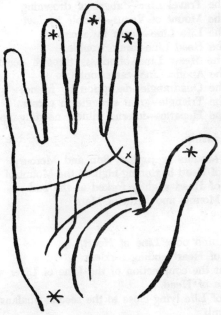

Helen Keller

Stars, Signs from

On the Mount of Mercury—loss by theft or treachery.
On the Mount of Apollo—fame by chance.
On the Mount of Saturn—accident or misfortune.
On the Mount of Jupiter—family trouble.
On the Mount of Mars (under Mercury)—death in battle or assassination.
On the Mount of Mars (under Jupiter)—litigation
On the Plain of Mars—railway accident.
On the Mount of Luna—sign of illness.
On the Travel Line—danger of drowning.
On the Mount of Venus—trouble by love.
On the Life Line—death by accident.
On the Head Line—brain trouble.
On the Heart Line—blindness through accident.
On the Apollo Line—catastrophe
On the Quadrangle—deception by friend.
On the Triangle—great struggle in career.
On the Hepatica—internal illness needing operation.

Statesmanship

Fine Mounts of Jupiter, Sun and Mercury.
Line of Head beginning high on the Mount of Jupiter.
Line of Head slightly forked at the end.
Fine Mounts and Plain of Mars.

Sterility

Weak and poor Line of Heart.
Line of Heart ending forkless.
Star at the conjunction of the Line of Liver and the Line of Head.
Line of Life lying close to the second phalanx of the thumb.
Cross on the Mount of Saturn.

Stock-Broker's Hand

Hand Spatulate.
Straight Line of Head.
Fingers of Saturn and Apollo equal,

Stoicism

Stoicism is indicated by a normal-sized Lower Mount of Mars on a hand with conical fingers.

Stomach Trouble

The Line of Head very thin.

Striking a Balance

The success of hand-reading is a matter of combination. The type of the subject must be combined with its energy, brain power, good intentions, vices, health conditions, and other important factors before striking a balance.

—*William G. Benham*

Subconscious Mind

In the plantigrade animals the palm constitutes the greater part of the hand; the palm of the plantigrade monkey, for instance, is far longer than its fingers. From this observation he (Carl Gustav Carus) concluded that human beings with unusually long palms have atavistic features of character. And he made the generalization that the palm is the index of the subconscious, and the fingers developing parallel with thought, the index of the conscious mind.

—*Charlott Wolff*

Success by Chance

A good Line of Fate with a star on the Mount of Sun.

Successful Ambitious Career

Line of Fate ending on the Mount of Jupiter.
Mount of Mars excellent.
Mount of Sun well-developed.
Mount of Mercury good.
Good Line of Liver.
Line of Fate long.
Line of Sun well-shaped.
Line on first finger from tip to base.
Line of Life starting from the Mount of Jupiter.
Life Line throwing branches into the Mount of Jupiter.
Well-proportioned hand.
Thumb excellent.

Successful Clerk

Knotted joints with conical fingers.

Success in Arts

A straight clear line from the Line of Head to the root of the third finger.

Success, Line of

The Line of Success or Sun is as the Sun is to the Earth; whenever it appears on the hand it promises brightness, success, and increase of fortune. Its best position is rising from the wrist to the base of the third finger.

—*Cheiro's* SECRETS OF THE HAND

Success, Signs of

Clear Line of Liver.
Long Line of Sun.

Line of Fate ending on the Mount of Jupiter or Sun.
Strong thumb.
Fine Mounts of Jupiter, Sun and Mercury.
Straight long Line of Head.

Success Through Hard Work

The first bracelet on the Rascette chained.
The Line of Sun rising from the Triangle.

Suicidal Mania

The Line of Head when sloping under the base of the Mount of Luna is a much more positive indication of acute suicidal mania than when the Line of Head curves downward into the face of the Mount of Luna.

—*Cheiro's* LANGUAGE OF THE HAND

Suicidal Tendencies

The excessively drooping Line of Head.
Conic or pointed hand.
Line of Head closely connected with the Line of Life.
Depressed Mount of Jupiter.
Very fully developed Mount of Saturn.
Many bars on the Line of Life.
Poor Line of Fate.
Line of Head merging into the Line of Liver.
Stars on the Mounts of Saturn and Moon.
Mount of Moon prominent.
Drooping Line of Head.

Suicide

A star on the Mount of Moon.
The Line of Head joined to the Line of Liver.
An exaggerated Mount of Jupiter.
An exaggerated first phalanx of the second finger.

Sunstroke

An island on the Line of Head under the Mount of Sun.

Superstition

Drooping Line of Head.
Exaggerated second finger.
Exaggerated Mount of Saturn.
Exaggerated Mount of Moon.

Surgeon's Hand

Long fingers.
Second knot developed in all the fingers.
Firm palm.
Head Line clear and deep.
"Science Lines" (called Medical stigmata) on Mercury.

Suspicion

A person with waving hands is of suspicious character. He sizes up everything and makes mental notes of all his surroundings.

Swindler

Mount of Moon exaggerate.
Line of Head deeply forked.
Long hand.
Crooked fingers.
Mounts wretched.

Syphilis

Syphilis is shown by an abnormal prominence of the Lower Mount of Mars or when it is criss-crossed by confused lines.

THE DICTIONARY OF PALMISTRY 213

Mount of Mercury exaggerated.
Mount of Mercury marked by confused lines.
Cross or star on the Mount of Mercury.

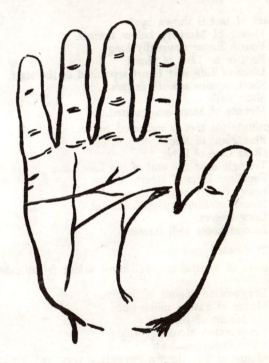

Eugenic Sandow

T

Tact

Lack of tact is shown by:
  Mount of Mercury below normal.
  Fourth finger unusually long.
  Poor or no Line of Heart.
  Lines of Life and Heart separated at the start.
  Short, square smooth fingers.
  Short nails.
  Mounts of Mars exaggerated.

Aptitude for tact is indicated by:
  Fine Plain of Mars.
  Good Line of Liver.
  Triangle near the end of the Life Line.
  Excellent Line of Heart.
  Long shapely second finger.
  Mount of Mercury predominant.
  Long fingers.
  Second knots well formed

Talent Abused

Misuse of artistic or intellectual talent is indicated by:
  Exaggerated Mount of Saturn.
  Mount of Saturn much lined.
  No Mount of Jupiter.
  Exaggerated Mount of Moon.
  Third finger crooked.
  Mount of Sun thrown towards a very bad Mount of Mercury.

Talking of Palmistry

An amateur palmist should stress rather the good that he sees than pointing out evil signs. It takes a very tactful person to point out faults without injuring the feelings of the subject.

Do not speak like this: You have enough ability to make several fortunes during your lifetime. You have also a great love of the people. You may not make the fortunes, because your drive is not in that direction, but you will get a great deal of happiness.

Speak rather like this: You have a great ability, but you will do nothing with it. You will let your love of people stand in your way.

Do not expound signs of ill-health blatantly. Rather say: I think it would be wise for you to guard your health carefully.

Talking of Talent

A great talented fame is indicated by one single line ending in a star on the Mount of Sun.

Tassel

A line ending in a tassel denotes weakness and destruction. It shows decay of power in old age.

Teaching Profession

Fine Lines of Head and Heart.
Lines of Life and Head slightly separated at the start.
Fine Mount of Sun.
Mounts of Jupiter and Venus well-marked.
Mounts of Mercury and Mars predominant.
Long, well-shaped thumb.
Square-tipped knotted fingers.

Teeth Trouble

Exaggerated Mount of Saturn.
Mount of Saturn much lined.
Long and wavy Line of Liver.
Long and wavy Line of Fate.

Exaggerated Mount of Saturn.
Mount of Saturn much lined.

Telepathic Powers

When the Line of Intuition forms a triangle with the Line of Fate and the Line of Head, it indicates a great command of the occult and telepathic powers.

Temper, Evenness of

When palm is resting upon the palm, it is an indication of repose and evenness of temper.

Temper Test

There are no surer indications of character than the nails and it is odd that they have not been more fully treated in books. To look at a person's nails is a useful way of confirming one's theories. It is particularly useful as a test of temper.

—*Henry Frith*

Temporary Mental Derangement

Thinness of a small portion on the Line of Head.

Tendencies

Palmistry indicates tendencies and not stubborn laws. All handicaps indicated in your hand can be overcome through persistence and proper action. Good indications, on the contrary, may be spoiled through indolence and inaction.

Texture of Fingers

Remember that smoothness is not practical, but knots are. Smoothness gives intuition or inspiration and an artistic taste, while knots show a practical, orderly, reflective, reasonable nature. These traits govern the hand according to the proportion in which they exist, and they must be considered to that extent.

—*Henry Frith*
PRACTICAL PALMISTRY

Thickness of Hand, Qualities of

Thick and hard—primitive rough nature.
Very thick and very hard—brutality.
Thick but not hard—kindly worker.
Thick and soft—self-indulgence and laziness.
Thick and not very soft—capacity for enjoyment.
Thick and very soft—Sensual nature.
Thin and very soft—heartlessness.
Thin and hard—selfishness.
Thin and soft—weak constitution.

Thief

Indications of an habitual thief are:
  Few lines on the hand.
  No Mount of Jupiter.
  Mount of Moon bulging.
  Mount of Mercury exaggerated.
  Crooked fingers.
  Mount of Mercury crossed or starred.
  Heavy elementary hand.

Third Finger, Qualities of

Too short—love of money.
Too long—speculation.
Fair size—prudence.
Crooked—false artistic sense.
Leaning towards the second—Morbid vanity.
Leaning towards the fourth—commercial art.
Longer than the first—unambitious love of art.
Equal to the first—great desire for fame.
Shorter than the first—blind ambition.

Equal to the fourth finger—great power for good and evil.
Unusually longer than the fourth finger—success in arts.
Shorter than the second finger—failure everywhere.
Equal to the second finger—gambling instinct.
Longer than the second—desperate risks.

Thoughtless Disposition

Mount of Mercury absent or insignificant.
High Mount of Moon.
Wide space between the Lines of Life and Head.
Wide space between base of second and third fingers.

Thought-Reading

A whorl on the Mount of Moon gives a person the uncanny ability to read the mind and motives of others. It gives foresight into the coming events. It assures flashes of keen understanding into life and literature.

Three Worlds of Palmistry

The Three Worlds of Palmistry are represented by the Fingers, the Upper Palm and the Lower Palm These represent mental, abstract, and material element respectively. If the fingers predominate, the subject's sphere is mainly mental. If the middle portion of the hand is more pronounced, the subject excels in ambition, shrewdness, wisdom, prudence, aggression. The development of the lower portion of the hand highlights the cultivation of meaner motives, directed towards the gratification of gluttony, sensual desires and coarse enjoyments. A hand with the three worlds equally developed represents a bright and balanced nature.

Throat Trouble

Thin, brittle and long nails.

Thumb

The superiority of man over animals lies in the hand, his superiority over other men in the thumb.

—*Aristotle*

The thumb individualizes the man.

—*D'Adpentigny*

In India the thumb is the centre and foundation of the Hindu system of Palmistry.

—*Cheiro*

Lacking the necessary proofs, a study of the fingers, particularly the thumb of man, would convince me of the existence of God.

—*Sir Isaac Newton*

It has been said that God gave man a mind and thumb, so that he can think and build.

—*Frances Kienzle*

Thumbs, Divisions of

These three factors so strongly estimated are Will, Power and Determination (indicated by the first phalanx), Reason and Logic (indicated by the second) and Love and Sympathy (indicated by the third or the Mount of Venus). Thus it will be seen that in the thumb, we have the determination backed by reason, and forced on by love, which is a combination so strong that will overcome any obstacles which may seek to impede its progress, and will often force success which with such an outcome seems impossible.

—*William G. Benham*

Thumb, Importance of

Gipsies in their judgment of character make the

TENDANCY TO HEART TROUBLE   **TENDANCY TOWARDS PARALYSIS**

THROAT AFFCTIONS   **BRONCHIAL**   **DELICASY OF LUNGS**

DELICASY OF LUNGS   **SPECIAL WEAKNESS**   **BAD CIRCULATION**

thumb the greatest foundation for all their remarks. Being interested with gipsies in my early life, I know this for a fact, for I have seen and watched them from the position, angle and general appearance of the thumb make their calculations accordingly. In India they have a variety of systems by which they read the hand, but here, again, they make the thumb the centre and foundation, no matter what system they work out. The Chinese also believe in Palmistry, and they, too, base their remarks on the position of the thumb itself.

—Cheiro

Thumb Lines, Readings from

Cross near the nail—unchastity.
Short lines near the nail—legacies.
Lines crossed—great obstacles.
Downward lines—will power.
Triangle—philosophic talent.
Square—unshakable logic.
Grille—acute moral sense.
Girdle—triumph of reason.

Thumb, Qualities of

High—lack of adaptability.
Too high—idiocy.
Low—generosity.
Close to the fingers—greed.
Away from fingers—extravagance.
Long—fine capacity for thoughtful action.
Very long—obstinacy.
Short—weak reasoning.
Very short—fickleness.
Flexible—unconventionality.
Bending back—generosity.
Stiff—stubbornness.
Slender—refined nature.

Broad—violent outbursts.
Flat—nervousness.
Thick—rough nature.
Large—practical life.
Small—sentimentality.

Time, Determination of

The clockwork of hand determines time of life, fate and fortune, accident and death, with fair correctness. Time can be approximated by observation, study and analysis of various lines, their location, and development, their strength and weakness.

Timidity

Narrow Quadrangle Line of Head attached a pretty far with the Line of Life at the start.
Mounts of Mars, Mercury and Jupiter very low.
Thin, soft palm.
Long knotted fingers bent inward.

Tips and Knots, Indications from

Knotted fingers with square tips—science, logic and Mathematics.
Knotted fingers with spatulate tips—love of locomotion, engineering or mechanical activities.
Knotted fingers with pointed tips—practical nature.

Tragedy, Comic

Charlie Chaplin is the King Comedian of today. His hand bears the Line of Comic Tragedy. According to Josef Ranald who examined his hands:—

"The Line of Comic Tragedy starts at the bottom of the palm from the termination of what is known as the Line of Life and rising upwards, terminates in a small triangle underneath the second finger. It signifies a nature that is somewhat gloomy in its outlook, with a genius for portraying the droller side of life."

Traitor

Line of Heart absent.
Short and pale nails.
Crooked fingers.

Traveller, Habitual

Square palm.
Hand thick and elastic.
Short spatulate fingers.
Third finger pronounced.
Fine Mounts of Sun and Moon.
Deep straight Line of Head.
A line from Rascette straight up to the Mount of Jupiter.

Travel Lines

There are two distinct ways of telling travels and voyages. One is from heavy lines on the face of the Mount of Luna. The other is from the little hair-lines that leave the Line of Life but travel on with it.

Ending on the Mount of Jupiter—great power and position promised through a very long journey.
Ending in islands—material loss due to journey.
Ending in a square—protection from danger in a journey.
Ending with a small cross—journey causing disappointment.
Ending on the Mount of Mercury—sudden death.
Ending on the Mount of Apollo—riches and fame.
Ending on the Mount of Saturn—fatality will dominate the journey.

Triangle

A triangle is an indication of great mental brilliancy with respect to the line and place where it occurs.

Triangle of Ready Wit

The Triangle of Ready wit is found beneath the fourth finger. It is a symbol of ready wit and daring talk.

Triangle, Smaller

The Smaller Triangle is formed by the Lines of Life, Head and Fate. Many hands have only the Smaller Triangle The Great Triangle is not usually visible on most of the hands.

Triangles, Signs from

"Triangles are favourable signs and show an aptitude for scientific pursuits."
On the Mount of Venus—worldly wisdom.
On the Mount of Luna or Moon—Intuition.
On the Mount of Jupiter—diplomatic career.
On the Mount of Mars—military honours
On the Mount of Mercury—success in science.
On the Mount of Apollo—success in medicine.
On the Mount of Saturn—occult.

Triangle, The Great

The Great Triangle is formed by the Line of Life, the Line of Head and the Line of Liver. When the Line of Liver is missing, it should be supplied by the imagination. It is also called the Plain of Mars. The following indications should be noted about the Great Triangle:—
Very broad and well-shaped—generosity.
Clear with deep pink lines—good understanding.
Flat—meanness.
Badly formed—avarice.
Crescent in the triangle—faithfulness.
Triangle within the triangle—military honours.
Heavy and pale—materialism.

Trident

A trident is a three-pronged spearhead. It is a favourable indication. It increases chances of success by adding strength and brilliance.

Troubles in Love

A star inside the Triangle.
A chained Line of Fate crossing the Line of Heart.

Troubles in Manhood

The Line of Fate poorly marked in the centre.

Tumour, Cancer

Head Line turning up
Islands on the Hepatica.

Typhoid

Black or bluish dot on the Line of Heart.
Dark dots on the Line of Head.
Broken Line of Liver.
Line of Liver very narrow.
Line of Liver highly coloured.
Bluish dot on the Line of Life.

Tyrannical Disposition

The Line of Heart often absent.
Deep straight Line of Head crossing the hand like a bar.
Exaggerated Mount of Jupiter.
First phalanx of the thumb exaggerated.
Long, hard nails.
First finger too long.

U

Unconventionality

Lines of Life and Head separate at the start.
Thumb set very low.
Thumb curved backward.
Fingers smooth and conical.
Fingers bent backward.
All fingers falling apart easily.
Thick soft palm.
Mounts of Sun, Moon and Venus predominant.

Unhappiness Through Women

A star on the base of the Mount of Venus just below the second phalanx.

Unhappy Marriages, Prevention of

When we can prevent the marriage of people whose temperaments make it absolutely impossible that they should live harmoniously, then we shall have largely decreased the number of divorces and wrecked lives. To do these things manifestly requires that we should have a correct estimate of the person with whom we are dealing.

—*William G. Benham*

Unsociability

When the hand is very white, almost deathlike pale, it indicates a cold indifference of temper. Such people are unsocial, have a flabby heart, and make good critics of destructive nature.

Unusual Shrewdness

When a crooked finger of Mercury is seen on any hand, the thought of unusual shrewdness should at once come to the mind, and you should be on your guard and search for everything that will tell whether actual dishonesty exists or not. Having located a Mercurian subject, and finding a crooked finger of Mercury, be on your guard to investigate at once for actual dishonesty. This applies to whatever station in life your subject may occupy. If his position be high, you know that the temptation to overstep the line of honesty has often been great even though resisted. With this crooked finger and the bad signs, feel sure that he will not resist very stubbornly.

—*William G. Benham*

Upper Mars, Qualities of the Mount of

Normal—Martyr's courage, patriotism, soldier, explorer.
Above Normal—Religious prosecutor, wounded vanity, violent disappointment, roguery.
Below Normal—Coward in creed, public shyness, cowardice.

V

Vacillation

Vacillation of mind and mood is indicated by: Lines of Fate and Sun forked and accompanied by:—

Short wavy sister lines.
Plain of Mars low.
Soft palm.
Fingers smooth and spatulate.
First phalanx of thumb below normal.
Mount of Jupiter insignificant.
Lines of Head and Life attached a pretty distance.

Vanity

Exaggerated Mount of Jupiter
Exaggerated Mount of Sun
Third finger abnormally long.
Mounts of Venus and Moon exaggerated.
Line of Life forked at the start.
Third finger leaning towards the second.
Mount of Jupiter displaced towards the Mount of Saturn.

Variations of Hand

To learn to know the disposition, in the atmospheric variations of the hand, is a more certain study than that of physiognomy. Thus, arming yourself with this science, you arm yourself with a great power, and you will have a thread that will guide you into the labyrinth of the most impenetrable hearts.

—*Balzac*
LA COUSIN PONS

Vegetative Existence

Absence of the Mount of Saturn indicates a vegetative existence and an insignificant humdrum life.

Venereal Disease

Black spot on the Mount of Venus.
Star on the Girdle of Venus.
Double Girdle of Venus.

Venus, Girdle of

Girdle of Venus is a ring round the base of the second and third finger, encircling or cutting through the Mounts of Saturn and Apollo. It indicates an extremeness of character. The person is ready to go to any extremes for his ideas. He will not listen to others, if once he sees the clarity of his own purpose. It gives a person very great drive in life and makes martyrs. All crusaders require a determination which the Girdle of Venus alone gives.

The Girdle of Venus is called *L. Anneau de Venus* n French. Adrian Lesbarrolles, the French writer, praises it highly:—

"Passion being caused in most cases by a superabundance of animal, or rather, vital spirits, may be made use of to increase the magnetic influence emanating from these elect creatures whom we feel instinctively to be endowed with genius; it becomes like a devastating torrent which, between stone-hewn dams, ever kept in the strongest repairs, loses its power for evil and drives instead the wheels of work—and wealth—dispensing factories."

Venusian Type

A person with the Mount of Venus predominant is called the Venusian. He loves beautiful clothes, music and dance. He is extremely feminine and voluptuous. He has a magnetic personality. He is affectionate, warm, attractive and romantic. He has an aura of fascination round his head. He is at once the tempter and the tempted. He spins round the wheel of sexual force to a higher plane.

Venus, Qualities of the Mount of

Normal—Ideal love, material love of poetic character, honest family affection, sincere devotion.

Above Normal—Sensuous imagination, faithfulness, sensuality, having many sweethearts.

Below Normal—Above love affairs, artist wedded to art, indifference to sex, hatred for the opposite sex.

Versatility

Forked Head Line.
Palm shorter than fingers.
Fine long third and fourth fingers.
Beautiful Mounts of Sun and Mercury.
Line of Sun exceptionally good.

Via Lasciva

Via Lasciva or the Milky Way runs close along the palm, at the edge, opposite the Line of Life and usually acts as a sister line to the Line of Liver. It gives the subject a superabundance of energy. On a coarse and uncultivated hand, it is an added threat. To a high type of hand it adds a great promise.

Via Lasciva—Readings from

Deep and clear—sensuality.
Wavy and long—immorality.
Forked—wasting of wealth due to excessive extravagance.
Star—"Riches, but much trouble to secure them, keep them and enjoy them, due to exaggerated influence of and love for the opposite sex.

(The *Via Lasciva* runs parallel to the Line of Liver, starting from the Plain of Mars and ending on the Mount of Mercury).

Vice

Worst consequences of sexual vice are indicated by:
A pale wide Line of Heart.
Triple Girdle of Venus.
Mounts of Saturn and Venus exaggerated.
Mounts of Saturn and Venus much lined.

Vindictiveness

Often the Line of Heart entirely absent.
Line of Head crossing the hand like a bar.
Mounts and Plains of Mars exaggerated.
Very narrow Quadrangle.
Mount of Sun exaggerated.

Violent Nature

Deep and long line of the Mount of Mars.
Lines of the palm red in colour.
Exaggerated Mounts and Plain of Mars.
Nails long, thick and curved clawlike.
Hand thick and hard.
Reddish hair.
Very hairy hands.

V.I.P. Friendships

Friendships with the V.I.P.'s or "Very Important people" are indicated by one or two crosses on the second phalanx of the second finger.

Visionary

Mounts insignificant.
Drooping Line of Head
Hands thick and soft.

Fingers with pointed tips.
Palm longer than fingers.

Voyages, Lucky

Line from the Rascette to the Mount of Jupiter.
Horizontal lines along the Percussion.

Voyages, Unlucky

Broken, crossed, starred or islanded horizontal lines along the Percussion.
Two lines from the Rascette to the Mount of Saturn, crossing each other.

W

Wavering Mind

When a person cannot keep his hands steady, his emotions are not under control. He has a strong character but he is uncertain of his purpose.

Wealth and Honour

Branches rising from the Line of Life towards the centre of the Line of Head.

Where Cupid Dwells

The Mount of Venus is the Mount Pleasant where Cupid dwells. It signifies love, sensuality and passion. It shows a yearning for companionship. It houses a temple for worship of beauty in every form.

Whole and Sole Love

A cross on the Mount of Venus.
The Line of Heart evenly forked under the Mount of Jupiter.
A cross on the Mount of Venus.
The Line of Fate losing itself in the Line of Heart.

Wickedest Vice

If several lines rise from the *Via Lasciva* and cut the Head Line, the subject is capable of committing the vilest crimes, including rape, murder, arson, in getting his lascivious desires satisfied. A deep *Via Lasciva* with a strong Line of Mars, thick third phalanges and a big Mount of Venus will make him the very demon of a man. He will consume the world and himself in a towering, roaring passion.

Whorls

Every hand has some mysterious whorls. These are described by Mrs. Nellie Simmons in her book, *The Lion Paws*. These whorls are formed by capillaries in the skin pigment. These are shaped like the fingerprints.

"If you have any whorls in your hand, you are to be considered fortunate indeed."

—Rita Van Allen

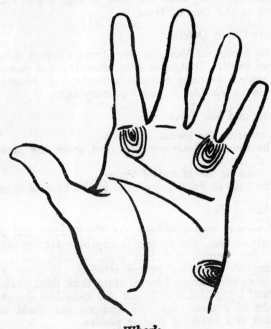

Whorls

Widowhood

The Line of Marriage slopping towards the Line of Heart.
The Line of Fate broken.
A line from the Line of Heart to the Line of Fate.
A black spot on the Line of Marriage.

Windfall

A windfall or sudden financial gain is indicated by:
   White spots on the Head Line under the Mount of Saturn.
   Fate Line rising from the Head Line.
   Fate Line ending on the Mount of Jupiter.
   A good Sun Line rising from a good Fate Line
   Fate Line ending with a star.
   A cross on the bracelet.

Wit and Humour

Wit and humour is indicated by the Mount of Mercury leaning towards the fourth finger.

Woman-Behind-Man Power

Mount of Venus insignificant.
Line of Heart poor
Drooping Line of Head.
Strong Mount of Moon.
Square palm.
Long knotty fingers.
Very short nails.
Lines red and deep.
The hand furrowed by cross lines.
Lines of Head and Life widely separated at the start.
Excessive Mounts of Jupiter and the Sun.

Woodrow Wilson, Hand of

The thumb of President Wilson's hand was low set, well-developed and well-formed at the tip. This gave him fine capacity for thought and action, indicating a genius for knowing when to go ahead, backed by sound judgment.

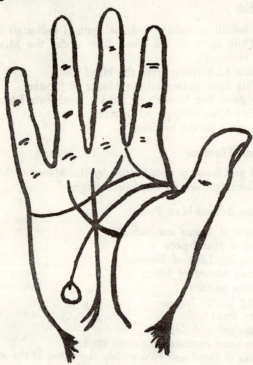

Woodrow Wilson

World of Childhood

If an influence line starts near the source of the Life Line and runs parallel to it, it represents the subject's mother on the presumption that her influence leaves an earlier impression than that of anybody else. The next line should be that of his father. If the child becomes an orphan early, these are guardians who brought him up.

Wounds

The Line of Head broken under the Mount of Saturn.
Spots on the Line of Head.

Wounds, Dangerous

Black dot on the Line of Life.
Lines from the first phalanx of the thumb to the Line of Life.

Wounds in a Fight

A spot on the Upper Mount of the Mars.

Wounds in Vital Organs

Very small lines on the Upper Mount of Mars.

Wounds, Mortal

Stars or breaks on the Line of Life, Head or Heart.
The signs above repeated in both hands.
Break or ominous sign on the Line of Fate.

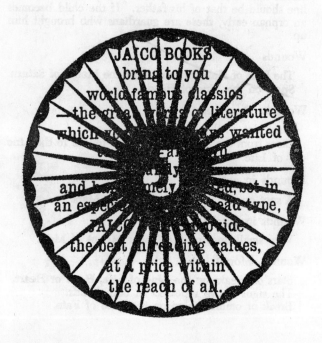